Also Authored by Debora J. McLaughlin

- *Running in High Heels: How to Lead with Influence, Impact, and Ingenuity*
- *The Renegade Leader: 9 Success Strategies Drive Leaders Use to Ignite People, Performance & Profits*

Co-Authored Titles by Debora J. McLaughlin

- *No Winner Ever Got There Without a Coach* with David Rock et al.
- *Straight Talk on Getting Results: Corporate America's 10 Most Respected Speakers and Trainers Speak Out* with Mona Pearl et al.
- *Roadmap for Career Success* with Lisa Martelli
- *Blueprint for Success: Proven Strategies for Success and Survival* with Ken Blanchard, Stephen R. Covey, et al.

CHANGE ABILITY

How to Navigate Change with Clarity, Confidence & Certainty

Debora J. McLaughlin

BALBOA.PRESS

A DIVISION OF HAY HOUSE

Balboa Press books may be ordered through booksellers or by contacting:

Balboa Press
A Division of Hay House
1663 Liberty Drive
Bloomington, IN 47403
www.balboapress.com
844-682-1282

Print information available on the last page.

ISBN: 979-8-7652-5224-6 (sc)
ISBN: 979-8-7652-5223-9 (hc)
ISBN: 979-8-7652-5222-2 (e)

Library of Congress Control Number: 2024909605

Balboa Press rev. date: 07/24/2024

"Debora McLaughlin has done it again and identified one of the critical skills organizations must master. *Changeability* is a guide for leaders seeking to elevate their strategy for growth and innovation while reducing the friction that change typically brings in their teams. As the Growth Architect, founder of 'The Women's Code,' and bestselling author of *Happy Woman Happy World,* I deeply appreciate Debora McLaughlin's approach to change and the adaptability required from us and our teams when we want to make a change. For anyone wanting to harness change as a catalyst for growth, *Changeability* is a must-read because it empowers leaders to navigate business transformation with agility and innovation while creating a healthy culture where your team is on board with your strategic goals."

— Beate Chelette, Growth Architect and author of
The Women's Code: Happy Woman Happy World

"*Changeability* stands as the cornerstone of successful strategy and innovation. The ability to adapt, pivot, and seize opportunities is paramount in a world characterized by rapid shifts and disruptive advancements. *Changeability* equips individuals and organizations with the tools to infuse strategic vision with agile execution. It fosters a culture where innovation thrives, barriers are dismantled, and creativity flourishes. By harnessing *Changeability's* power, leaders can confidently navigate uncertainty, embrace calculated risks, and drive transformational strategies that elevate their organizations above the competition. Debora's insights extend far beyond theories; they are rooted in real-world applications that yield tangible ROI results. Her unique ability to infuse change leadership, adaptability, and agility sets her apart as a guiding light for those navigating the uncharted waters of change."

— Lisa Ann Edwards
CEO, founder of Excelia.io

"*Changeability* is a remarkable guide that intersects seamlessly with the principles I've espoused in *Talent is a Team Sport*. Debora McLaughlin's insights are aligned with cultivating the right team and with a profound impact on customers when the right people are in place. With *Changeability*, leaders can navigate change confidently, ensuring their teams are adaptable and poised to create exceptional customer experiences that drive lasting success."

— Denise Graziano,
author of *Talent is a Team Sport*

"*Changeability* is a game-changer for leaders seeking to enhance their impact, presence, and visibility. As someone deeply immersed in media training and personal branding, I was captivated by how Debora McLaughlin emphasizes the essence of establishing a powerful presence. Her guidance empowers leaders to navigate change and confidently step into the spotlight. *Changeability* is a must-read for those ready to amplify their presence and create a lasting impact."

— Cheryl Tan, media trainer, and
personal branding expert

"Debora McLaughlin's insights effortlessly resonate with the heart of compassionate, collaborative, and authentic leadership. Her approach to change leadership mirrors the essence of fostering a culture where empathy and growth converge. *Changeability* empowers leaders to navigate transformation with a heart-centered, love-based leadership perspective, cultivating a workplace where individuals flourish and change becomes a shared journey. This book is an invaluable companion for those ready to harness change as a catalyst for embracing the human dimension of leadership."

— Dr. Maria Church,
author of *Love-Based Leadership: The Model for
Leading with Strength, Grace, and Authenticity*
and *A Course in Leadership: 21 Spiritual
Lessons on Power, Love, and Influence*

CONTENTS

Discover the transformative philosophy of Changeability and unlock the secrets to confidently navigating today's dynamic business landscape. Gain insights into harnessing change as a strategic advantage while understanding the evolution of your leadership role amidst technological disruptions and innovative opportunities.

Leading change is no longer enough; the modern leader is expected to proactively steer their organization through innovation and disruption. It's a journey that demands vision, courage, and an unwavering commitment to harnessing the power of change. Discover strategies for swiftly aligning your team and leveraging change leadership to deliver profound organizational transformation.

ACKNOWLEDGMENTS

First and foremost, my heartfelt appreciation goes out to my clients—the true heroes of this narrative. Your insights, challenges, and successes have woven a rich tapestry of experiences, breathing life into the concepts shared in this book. Each of you has played a crucial role in making these pages resonate with authenticity. I extend my deepest gratitude for your unwavering trust and for allowing your stories to be shared, inspiring others on their transformative paths.

I am indebted to my circle of friends and colleagues who lent a listening ear to my ceaseless struggles with finding the precise words and scenarios to paint the most explicit pictures of the concepts embedded within these pages. Your patience, insights, and support have been invaluable in shaping this work's final form.

Turning inward, I extend heartfelt thanks to my family—the unwavering pillars of support who shared my late-night encounters with the muse that beckoned ceaselessly. Your patience, understanding, and encouragement were the foundations that sustained me through this creative odyssey. Your unwavering belief in my purpose propelled me to capture the essence of *Changeability*.

Lastly, I thank those who have made this book's journey possible. I wouldn't start any writing endeavor without the guidance of Donna Kozik. Her writing programs and editorial direction spurred my momentum. Lastly, my publisher, Balboa Press, a division of Hay House, thank you for bringing my third book to life.

I extend my most profound appreciation to all those who have contributed to the creation of *Changeability* and supported me on this journey. This book is a tribute to our collective efforts, forging a path toward transformative change.

DEDICATION

This book is dedicated to the bold change leaders who fearlessly shape the future.

"In any given moment we have two options: to step forward into growth or step back into safety."
— Abraham Maslow

FOREWORD

As we stand on the brink of what promises to be an era of unparalleled transformation, I find myself reflecting on a belief that feels both exhilarating and somewhat daunting: we are poised to experience more change in the next decade than we have in the past century. This rapid acceleration, largely propelled by technological innovation and societal shifts, lays the groundwork for Debora J. McLaughlin's seminal work, *"Changeability: How to Navigate Change with Clarity, Confidence, and Certainty."*

I have heard it said so many times that the only thing that is constant is change. And that is true. But what is quite different about this era of change is its ever-increasing pace. Our ability to adapt to a complex and uncertain environment will be more critical now than ever. How might we shift our thoughts and behaviors in times of uncertainty? How we react and respond will be essential to our survival.

Companies are made of people and their thinking. In my book *Moonshot Innovation*, I stressed that to solve the challenges of today and tomorrow, we can no longer use the techniques, thinking, and processes of yesterday. We need to embrace opportunities from the fastest technological and innovative period in history—and it's only just begun.

I founded AQai to provide an operating system for

exponential change. Debora and I share the same passion for inspiring and preparing a new wave of exponential leadership, one that can lead us to an abundant, healthy, and thriving future.

Debora is a founding partner of the AQai community and serves on our Client Advisory Board. Since I have known Debora, she has had a passion for helping leaders, teams, and organizations achieve beyond what they believed to be possible. Her journey from the vibrant corridors of New York City to the tech-savvy streets of Boston is a testament to her passion for connecting people, resources, and organizations in novel and impactful ways. She realizes that change is unique to each individual and is not easy. There are stakeholders to engage, resources to be gained, and politics to navigate. She expertly addresses these challenges and more within the pages of "Changeability".

I have witnessed Debora's work within an organization. I am not surprised she wrote "Changeability" to share her insights, experience, and unique understanding of human dynamics. Using AQai data as her guide, she intuitively knows which skills to activate or amplify. She builds trust and safety to allow for experimentation and, through her effort, births hope, optimism, and confidence. Her clients not only gain business results, but they also become empowered for their future.

At the heart of "Changeability" lie the triumvirate virtues of clarity, confidence, and certainty. Clarity comes from a deep understanding of our environment, both internal and external, allowing us to discern the signals amidst the noise. Confidence is forged in the crucible of adaptability and resilience, empowering us to meet change head-on with an open heart and a steady hand. And certainty, paradoxically, lies in our acceptance of uncertainty, anchored in the belief in our ability to adapt and overcome.

Debora McLaughlin beautifully distills the essence of change leadership, adaptability, and agility—three pillars that underpin not just professional success but the very fabric of our lives in these turbulent times. It's about envisioning a future where we're not simply passive passengers but active pilots, guiding others with a clear vision and unwavering purpose. My own experiences resonate with this approach, having witnessed first-hand the transformative impact of visionary leadership that embraces change as an ally rather than an adversary.

I believe success is about the speed and grace with which we respond to change, a theme that finds its voice in the pages of "Changeability." McLaughlin's work deeply aligns with the concept of Adaptability Intelligence (AQ), advocating for a mindset where agility is a strategy and a state of being, empowering both individuals and organizations to leap ahead of the curve.

AQ highlights and measures the abilities, characteristics, and environmental factors that impact the successful behaviors of people and organizations to respond effectively to uncertainty, new information, or changed circumstances. As a leader, it gives you actionable insights you can leverage. Adaptability rewires our brains to escape the destructive cycles that keep us trapped in the past, unable to embrace our future.

Debora's insights resonate enormously with my own journey, affirming that true leadership is not about holding onto power but empowering others to realize their potential in the face of change.

Importantly, this book delves into the myriad of ways adaptability can be nurtured and harnessed, echoing many of the insights I've shared in my work. It underscores the reality that adaptability is not a fixed trait but a muscle strengthened through continuous effort and reflection.

It is filled with real-world examples, case studies, and practical exercises to help you translate Changeability from information to transformative practice. Whether you are leading a small team or a large organization, facing incremental change or a profound disruption, Changeability will equip you with what you need to succeed.

One analogy I have found particularly helpful when dealing with dizzying change is this: When you play a video game, you usually begin with no map of territory. As you explore, the map expands. Each time you reach a new "edge," new territory reveals itself. We are still determining what our new map looks like. It can end up being more expansive than you ever imagined.

I invite you to step into the unknown, and no matter what map appears, you can navigate it with clarity, confidence, and certainty of your win.

As you turn these pages, embrace Changeability as a guide and a gateway to mastering the art of navigating rapid change. The path is paved with the choices we make, the challenges we embrace, and the future we dare to imagine. Here's to becoming architects of change in a world that awaits our vision, our voice, and our valor.

Ross Thornley
Author, *Moonshot Innovation* and *Decoding AQ*
Founder, AQai.io

CHAPTER 1

Introduction

The future isn't scary if you are the one creating it.
—Debora J. McLaughlin

T he success or failure of an organization often hinges on its ability to navigate and thrive amidst change. As a change leader, you're at the forefront of this transformative journey, steering your team and organization toward a brighter future. But what if you had access to a roadmap that not only demystifies the complexities of change but also empowers you to become a true architect of transformation? What if you could unlock the secrets to not just managing change but harnessing its limitless potential to elevate your leadership and your organization to unprecedented heights?

Your role as a leader is to lead, drive, and deliver change.

Yet, successfully delivering on change and innovation can be challenging. You may be facing the same challenges as many of my clients. Challenges such as resistance to change, a lack of buy-in and support from stakeholders, resource constraints, conflicting priorities, and the complexities of implementing change in a dynamic environment can become everyday speedbumps. On top of that, there are communication hurdles, team dynamics, and navigating through intricate organizational structures.

But what if you possessed the power of Changeability?

Many leaders confide in me that they lie awake at night, worrying about the success of their organization or team's ability to navigate change. The decisions required to improve the bottom line, respond to global trends, address customer needs, and optimize team dynamics can be overwhelming. You might have a high-stakes project, whether a digital transformation, launching a new product or service, maximizing customer satisfaction, or streamlining departmental operations for greater efficiency. The competition is relentless, and there's a constant expectation to move forward faster with fewer resources.

The fear of being wrong, facing backlash, or even losing

your job and reputation can be daunting. However, your future success relies not only on you but also on your team's performance.

Change is inevitable. But the ability to adapt, anticipate, and lead change is not. Those who cling to outdated paradigms risk becoming irrelevant, while those who embrace change position themselves at the forefront of innovation and opportunity.

Within the pages of *Changeability*, you'll leave behind these worries, emerging as a leader who guides change with clarity, confidence, and certainty. Imagine gaining quicker support from stakeholders. Picture having a team that takes responsibility and is genuinely motivated by change, leading to improved outcomes. Envision becoming your organization's trusted leader for pushing boundaries and achieving progress. All of this is possible.

I define Changeability as the capacity of individuals, teams, and organizations to effectively adapt, evolve, lead, and initiate shifts, challenges, and opportunities.

Changeability represents the willingness and proficiency to embrace change as a catalyst for growth, learning, and innovation. It encompasses a flexible mindset, agile strategies, and a proactive approach to navigating today's dynamic landscape. With this foundational skill set, leaders and teams strengthen their ability to respond to change and share and capitalize on it, ensuring sustainable success.

By cultivating Changeability within yourself and your team, you are not merely surviving the turbulence of change but harnessing it. You not only turn obstacles into opportunities, but you also identify pathways for growth, ensuring that you remain proactive rather than reactive in a future that waits for no one.

My mission is to ignite the spark of possibility thinking in each individual, empowering them to turn their visions into reality.

In a world where the mere mention of change often conjures feelings of becoming overwhelmed, hesitating, or guarded excitement, I invite you to embark on a journey that disrupts the notion of change and your role within it.

Let's get started.

CHAPTER 2

Unleashing the Power of Changeability

"Many organizations and managers are struggling to stay afloat and aligned in the volatile, uncertain, complex and ambiguous nature of today's global business environment. Turbulence—the rapid rate of change—is swirling around many of us, tipping us this way and that as we attempt to navigate a safe passage through it all."

**—Paul Kinsinger,
Thunderbird School of Global
Management**

"I Need a Pen."

"I need a pen," he said. I noticed the tone of frustration in his voice before I saw the couple. The man who spoke was tall, dressed in a gray suit, and wore freshly polished shoes. He held a phone in one hand and turned toward the woman beside him. She wore a black beaded dress, with her hair curled into a wide braid across her head. The wedding reception had just begun, and people were moving into the large ballroom as I passed the couple in the hallway. "I need a pen," he said more firmly this time. I heard his pager buzzing urgently. "I have to call this patient back, and I need to write down what they need," he said as he felt inside his inner jacket, pushing his hand into the inner corner of its seams. He looked confused as his hand returned empty. Turning to her, she searched for a pen in her small handbag. Dressed for the wedding, she only carried her wallet, phone, brush, and lipstick. "I don't have a pen," she said. "Why don't you call them back and note on your phone what they need?" He looked at her and said firmly. "I always write it down; I need a pen."

As an avid observer of human behavior, I couldn't help but see this as an example of a person grappling with the need to do things differently than what he is accustomed to; he "always writes it down."

I suspect if I scanned the room, I might find someone else using their phone to pay their babysitter, transfer bank funds to their child for gas money, google the latest research to support their side of a disagreement at their table, record and transcribe a conversation or even use artificial intelligence to craft a ready response to a burning question.

The distinction between individuals who readily embrace change and those who don't often lies in their view of change. Those open to change tend to have an open mindset toward learning and are curious. They are adaptable, adjusting their routines to incorporate new tools, and are comfortable with uncertainty. They possess a positive attitude towards change, viewing it as an opportunity for growth, and see change as a means to solve problems. On the other hand, those who resist change, such as technological change, might view learning new ways of working as burdensome and prefer familiar methods, even if less effective.

Our natural inclination is to seek safety and stability. This primal instinct was ingrained for generations, a survival mechanism that has enabled us to thrive in an ever-evolving environment. Yet, this same instinct often becomes a barrier when navigating change in the modern world.

The prevailing narrative portrays change as something that happens to you, a force to adapt to in the name of safety. However, what if this perspective only offers a partial truth? But what if beneath this veil of apprehension lies a latent power? One that transcends the craving for safety.

What if change was normal, not a hurdle but a stepping stone to something better?

From my experience, I've seen an untapped dimension to this story, one where we possess the tools and resources needed to harness change as an advantage. It's an evolutionary advantage that enabled our ancestors to adapt, innovate, and thrive in the face of new environments and challenges. With our modern knowledge and technology resources, why wouldn't this same trait serve us today?

We are wired for safety, yet we are also wired for change.

How do I know? Experience with my clients has shown me this propensity many times. When clients realize they have an innate skill set for change, they see obstacles as opportunities.

They find possibility in what was once impossible. They come alive with excitement, and teams, once siloed, become cohesive. I've noticed what makes the difference between the leaders and teams who excel through change and those who struggle. It is their Changeability.

I developed Changeability to address the common challenges when confronting change, including procrastination, overthinking, and an unspoken belief that goals are unattainable. I've witnessed the erosion of teams who experience reduced emotional well-being and high work stress and feel siloed from their team and disconnected from their company. They couldn't see a path forward. They found it difficult to imagine a new reality. They failed to tap into the innate skills needed to bridge the gap from where they were to where they wanted to be until they discovered the framework of Changeability.

Like a refined recipe, I determined the critical ingredients needed to form the framework of Changeability. Like most great recipes it is simplistic and with three key components:

Change Leadership

Change Leadership: Change Leadership is the foundational core of Changeability and represents the ability to envision, lead, drive, and ultimately deliver change. It encompasses the skills and mindset required to navigate the complexities of change and effectively guide individuals and organizations toward a desired future state. Great change leaders inspire and motivate others, communicate a compelling vision, and mobilize resources to initiate and sustain transformational initiatives.

Adaptability

The second pillar of Changeability is adaptability. Adaptability is the capacity to both initiate and respond to change. It involves being open-minded, embracing new ideas and perspectives, and proactively seeking opportunities for growth and improvement. Adaptable individuals and organizations possess the resilience and flexibility to navigate uncertainty, adjust strategies as needed, and swiftly capitalize on emerging opportunities. They view change as a catalyst for innovation and continuously learn and evolve in response to dynamic environments.

Agility

Agility is the third pillar of Changeability and represents the ability to align, assess, and activate change with speed and scale. It encompasses the capacity to quickly identify and prioritize change initiatives based on their strategic importance, organizational impact, and resource availability. Agile individuals and organizations excel in executing change initiatives rapidly, efficiently, and effectively. They leverage streamlined processes, nimble decision-making, and a collaborative mindset to adapt to evolving circumstances and, as a result, deliver outcomes with exceptional speed and precision.

My experience partnering with change leaders led me to identify how, like a three-legged stool, change will falter without the support of all three. Together, these three pillars of Changeability form a robust framework for driving successful change and fostering a culture of innovation and growth.

The dimensions of Changeability might not be unfamiliar. What I find to be unknown is the mindset, skills, and abilities required under each. Skills such as mental flexibility, an innovative mindset, combined with resilience, adaptability, and grit top the list.

With over two decades of experience collaborating with change leaders, teams, and organizations, I've noticed something missing. They were often unaware of their change-ready skills or how to leverage them. These latent skills were not absent; they merely awaited discovery, activation, or amplification.

When you implement the framework of Changeability, you will build your capacity for change and that of your team. By identifying and embracing your inherent capabilities, you will recognize the qualities to transform yourself from a change navigator into a change leader. Your team will not only navigate change but also boldly lead and initiate it.

Imagine a paradigm where obstacles become opportunities, uncertainties are met with adaptability, and challenges are catalysts for growth. *Changeability* embodies this mindset, with the tools to navigate change confidently and foster teams that thrive amid shifting tides.

By cultivating Changeability within yourself and your team, you're not merely surviving these transitions but turning them to your advantage. This readiness to transform isn't just about safeguarding against challenges; it's about seizing the promise of what lies ahead, turning potential disruptions into avenues for growth, and ensuring that you remain proactive rather than reactive in a future that waits for no one.

Why does Changeability matter?

Unlike anything seen in the past century, the next decade promises unprecedented change. Given this impending transformation, it's crucial to consider how this seismic shift will impact those leading the charge for change.

I recently co-facilitated a forum, "Predictions: Building for 2030." We discussed predictive trends, and participants brainstormed how their organizations would prepare for these possible changes and how they might leverage them.

Topics of interest included artificial intelligence, cyber security, virtual reality, 3-D printed clothing and organs, a shift in wealth, currency, and many healthcare and technological innovations. We also looked at 2040 and 2050 predictions. Many were eye-opening.

As a leader in this re-imagined world, you face the exhilarating task of guiding your organization through the waves of innovation. You understand that staying ahead of the curve and harnessing the power of emerging technologies can unlock new opportunities and fuel growth. However, leading in this dynamic environment requires more than just embracing technology. It demands a strategic mindset, a visionary outlook, and the ability to inspire and mobilize your team.

Changeability, which encapsulates these essential elements of change leadership, adaptability, and agility, is the bedrock of building for the future. It's not merely an abstract concept; it's a practical necessity in an era where change is the only constant. It will not only offer you the skills needed, but it will also position you for your future.

Strengthening Change Capacity: Unleash Your Leadership Potential

Whether you're an innovator, change catalyst, or thought leader, the call to elevate your game is ever-present. But what's behind this growing need to sharpen our ability to navigate change effectively? The recent "State of the Organization 2023" report underscores the imperative for leaders and organizations to cultivate and fortify their change capacity.

Profound shifts, from technological advancements to the pressing demand for diversity, equity, and inclusion, underscore the importance of Changeability. Aligning business objectives with the dynamic needs of employees and consumers demands swift responsiveness. Meeting these evolving demands necessitates not only expanding your skill set but also attracting talent with the expertise to bridge capability gaps.

Resilience tops the list of essential capabilities. Resilient companies consistently yield a fifty percent greater return to their stakeholders compared to their less resilient counterparts. However, it's not merely about reacting to change; it's about having the mindset and leadership acumen to proactively lead and initiate change, propelling progress forward.

In today's landscape, you're not just expected to navigate change; you're required to spearhead it. Shockingly, a mere twenty-five percent of surveyed organizations believe they possess leaders capable of this proactive leadership style.

Unlock your potential with Changeability, a hallmark of effective leadership. Over eighty percent of my clients have experienced career advancements within a year of working together. Why? Because they are leaders who drive results. They motivate their teams, solve intricate problems, and identify growth opportunities. By showcasing your Changeability skill set, you not only build confidence in your leadership but also fortify your employment security.

How ready is your team or organization to face upcoming change?

Employees look to their leaders as their models for change leadership. A Jacob Morgan study asked managers and senior leaders if they felt prepared for upcoming trends. Sixty-one percent of leaders responded "yes, definitely."

Yet when individual contributors were asked about their confidence in their leaders' abilities, only twenty-one percent said they thought their leaders were prepared. There is a forty percent gap between how leaders viewed their change readiness and how employees viewed their readiness. Changeability allows you to build and demonstrate your leadership, increasing your team's confidence in your ability to lead and in their ability to lead, navigate, and initiate change.

A Passion for Change

I love working with driven visionary leaders who have the foresight to see what is possible. They watch for trends, predict the future and view disruption as an opportunity for innovation. These leaders exemplify the power of curiosity and a forward-thinking mindset.

I've always been a curious person.

Let me share a formative story. My bangs were cut across my forehead with that "bowl cut" of the home haircut done at the kitchen table. I wore my favorite black patent shoes with pants legs that were starting to rise despite my short stature. I looked at my mother and pondered her statement.

"If you keep talking, you will run out of words. You were only given so many words in life."

It was true.

I talked constantly, questioning everything around me. I asked "why" more times than the typical six-year-old. I also questioned every response. It was the questioning that I suspect bothered my parents the most. I never took anything at face value. I wondered how decisions were made and why other alternatives were not considered. I asked what was possible if another choice was made. It was endless.

As I pondered her question, believing it was true, I made a decision. It was worth it. Questioning what existed to see if anything else was possible was who I am. Even if I ran out of words.

As a consultant to leaders, teams, and organizations, I continue to ask questions. From an outside lens, I see what others need to see: the root of a problem or, even better, unforeseen potential ready to be unleashed.

Now, I hold the space for my clients to step to the edge of possibility. To make the risk worth it. Only from the edge of possibility do you see new opportunities.

I remember the day as if it were yesterday. As I sat in my psychology class, my gaze drifted beyond the window, and my professor's words faded into a distant hum. It was then that I sensed the world pulsating with excitement, just beyond the confines of my college campus. A transformation was underway—a technological revolution poised to reshape our lives. It was a symphony of opportunities, and I could feel its rhythm calling out to me.

During my junior year of college, I made a momentous decision that altered the course of my life. I chose to forgo the comforts of dorm living and the traditional college experience in exchange for a full-time career in technology. By day, I rode the relentless wave of technological change, while by night, I pursued my studies with unwavering dedication.

My journey began as employee number 38,997 at Digital Equipment Corporation, one of the most profitable technology companies in the United States, which grew to over fourteen billion dollars in revenue and over one hundred and twenty thousand employees.

Digital Equipment Corporation (DEC) was known for being at the forefront of innovation, constantly pushing the boundaries of what was possible. It birthed many of the technology leaders who later went on to leadership roles in other organizations. It held its place in the Fortune 500 for over twenty-five years, peaking at number twenty-seven.

Starting in logistics, I understood what was needed to provide products to our consumers; however, I quickly realized that my genuine interest was in partnering with organizations. I joined the sales team. I thrived on the excitement of introducing groundbreaking technology solutions, whether in the bustling skyscrapers of New York City or later in the vibrant tech scene of Boston, where I later joined a Fortune 500 telecommunications firm implementing solutions in Fortune 100 companies.

My corporate career spanned software, hardware, and telecommunications sales, and lastly, as a National Account Manager managing a team serving global clients. My position required building positive relationships with stakeholders of all levels. Senior executives, technology experts, department directors, legal, sales, and procurement leaders. Here, I honed my communication skills, customizing conversations to the priorities of diverse leadership functions.

Although coding proved challenging during my elective computer science class, and statistics felt like a never-ending maze, I discovered solace in leveraging my neuroscience and human dynamics education. Earning two master's degrees in psychology gives me insight to quickly understand people, their motivations, their worries, and how to unleash their potential.

Big ideas are born in conference rooms, think tanks, and innovation conferences worldwide. Leaders leave the room with enthusiasm about the new ideas expressed and how they will solve a problem or position an opportunity for growth or innovation. Or they leave the room with the plan to face a top challenge, defeat an obstacle, or navigate a new frontier. They are ready to do what is needed. Yet, I've often witnessed the enthusiasm and the ability to move forward diminish with each step down the hall, through Zoom meetings, or in the execution plans. Why? Because human dynamics slows it down. Their team members, already tired from their day-to-day work, want to avoid taking on another new project. Or they need their initiative resourced, and finance, legal, or accounting turns their head away, pointing to budget limitations already in place. Others believe the new idea is futuristic. A company President recently said his technology team said, "Artificial intelligence is just a fad." I responded, "Like the internet was?"

The truth is, not everyone is ready to embrace change. I am dedicated to helping leaders and teams look at change through a new lens.

People are the hub of all business. The human aspect of business, which I call the "people side," can be messy. As a leader, you encounter daily human dynamics challenges, communicating across the organization, motivating individuals, providing feedback, challenging perspectives, and aligning for core values. This "people side" of business captivated me. People can be the inspiration for innovation and also its barrier.

Throughout my tenure in the corporate world, I consistently observed a remarkable divergence between organizations characterized by their readiness to adopt new practices and those with a pronounced enthusiasm for embracing innovation. This divergence isn't just about technology adoption; it's a telling reflection of the level of their people's Changeability.

In organizations where technology adoption slowed, people resisted stepping out of established comfort zones. These entities often preferred to stick with tried-and-true methodologies, hesitant to disrupt their well-practiced routines. Such hesitancy often stemmed from a deep-rooted fear of the unknown, a reluctance to navigate the uncharted waters of change, and an aversion to stepping into the ambiguity that can accompany technological advancements.

On the other hand, the organizations that readily embraced innovation, incorporating new technologies enthusiastically, demonstrated a high degree of Changeability. They viewed technology not merely as tools but as enablers of progress. These entities were more adaptable, their teams demonstrating a willingness to adjust their processes to accommodate implementing new tools. The leaders within these organizations fostered a culture that actively encouraged learning, experimentation, and forward-thinking.

I realized my mission is to remove barriers to successful change.

Digital Equipment Corporation failed to evolve; it collapsed long after I had left the company due to its inability to remain relevant, to set trends instead of following them, and to let go of what had made it successful—the minicomputer. The company struggled to pivot toward the digital age, rapidly reshaping the technological landscape.

I share this story with you because I believe in your organization's potential to become truly exceptional, listed among the Good to Great organizations rather than featured in a later chapter of How the Mighty Fall.

For over 20 years, I have collaborated with forward-thinking leaders like yourself, their teams, and organizations who prioritize change and innovation to stay ahead in their industries. My clients strive to deliver the latest and best services, taking pride in their agility and speed. My work takes me across industries from healthcare, technology, insurance, government, finance, professional services, and manufacturing. My clients include an eclectic mix of leadership roles, from Chief Executive Officers and Chief Technology Officers to Chief Information and Digital Officers, all of whom are at the helm of pivotal tech strategy and implementation. In addition, I've partnered with professionals in Strategy, Risk Management, Innovation, Leadership, Training and Development, and other developmental leaders keen on driving transformational changes that influence business outcomes, customer satisfaction, and profitability. No matter the title, all were leaders—and you are, too.

These organizations understand that the business landscape is ever-evolving, and adaptation and innovation are crucial to remaining relevant. As a result, they do not settle for complacency and are open to new ideas, processes, and technologies. They do not only respond to change, they also create it.

Embrace Changeability for a Thriving Future

Changeability isn't just a buzzword or the latest workplace trend; it's the key to your career's success and your organization's survival. In today's fast-paced world, the ability to adapt, innovate, and thrive amidst constant change is not a luxury but a necessity for professional growth and advancement. With technology advancements, globalization, and rapid shifts becoming the norm, Changeability is no longer an option—it's a requirement for long-term success. Whether you're a leader, manager, or individual contributor, cultivating adaptability and resilience is essential to thrive in the evolving landscape of work.

Gain a Competitive Edge with Changeability

As a leader, the stakes are high; your team's performance, customer satisfaction, and business outcomes all depend on your leadership. Changeability empowers organizations to swiftly adapt to changing market dynamics, customer needs, and technological advancements, giving you a competitive edge. Whether you're launching an innovation, tackling talent attraction and retention, implementing a new back-to-work strategy, or optimizing the customer experience, Changeability is the driving force that sets you apart.

The Three Pillars of Changeability

Changeability's three integral pillars provide essential support for your leadership journey. Change leadership guides you through effective change management and communication, ensuring your team is engaged and aligned. Adaptability instills the mindset, mental flexibility, grit, and resilience necessary for readiness and progress. Agility adds speed and scale to your efforts, keeping priorities at the forefront. Together, these pillars foster innovation, learning from failure, unlearning old paradigms, and creating new possibilities.

Unlock Your Potential for Change

By embracing Changeability, you secure your employability and elevate your team's performance, bolstering your confidence and ability to deliver impactful results. In a world where change often elicits hesitation or guarded excitement, I invite you to embark on a transformative journey that redefines your relationship with change and your role in driving it. Let *Changeability* be your trusted roadmap, guiding you towards a future of continuous growth and success.

First, we begin with the mindset and skills of change leadership. Transforming your mindset from change-averse to change-forward represents a significant shift. With this shift, you move beyond simply navigating change. You actively steer its course, making your leadership a proactive force. The next chapter also offers a toolset you can immediately use to navigate obstacles, giving you the skills to influence others. This will result in a shift from thriving in change to actively shaping and influencing outcomes, even in the face of the unknown.

Next, we will look at the dimensions of adaptability, giving you and your teams insight into the skills that encompass the skills of adaptability. You'll gain a deeper understanding of how to harness your team's capabilities and pinpoint areas to bridge skill gaps effectively.

Lastly, as we explore the concept of agility, you'll learn how to infuse speed and scale into your approach, achieving results more swiftly and efficiently than ever before. These core chapters serve as a robust framework for nurturing a culture of change-readiness within yourself, your team, and your entire organization.

Get excited, your leadership journey is about to become easier.

CHAPTER 3

Change Leadership: Embrace Your Role as a Driver of Transformation

> *Change is the law of life. And those who look only to the past or present are certain to miss the future."*
>
> —John F. Kennedy

Dave and I were seated in his office, a cozy space with a window overlooking the bustling city. The air was stagnant, and I noticed his guest chair was well-worn. Dave's cluttered desk reflected the demands of his busy schedule, the papers telling stories of projects, deadlines, and a myriad of tasks. Dave's office served as the command center for his role as the Director of Technology. A seasoned professional, Dave had weathered his fair share of storms in the corporate world. His reputation as a change leader was renowned, and his peers often turned to him for guidance during times of upheaval. Reporting directly to the VP of Technology, Dave had built a team of exceptional individuals, all Prosci certified and equipped with the knowledge and skills gained from their certification and that of a Change Intelligence® program my company had delivered.

Confidence emanated from Dave as he spoke about his team's capabilities, their shared vision, and the extensive preparation they had undergone. Yet, beneath that veneer of confidence, I could detect a subtle undercurrent of anticipation and concern.

Dave's story struck a chord with me as he spoke. His story resembled those of many of the leaders I've partnered with. Dave was spearheading a digital transformation that spanned the entire enterprise. The organization sought to optimize operations, streamline processes, and drive efficiency by embracing cloud-based software solutions for various critical functions. From financial management to enterprise resource planning and human capital management to spending and supply management, the implications of this endeavor were immense and far-reaching.

The implications were clear—this digital transformation would touch the lives and work of every employee within the organization. As Dave meticulously outlined the scale and scope of the project, I could sense the magnitude of the task at hand. The ripple effect of the change would permeate through departments, teams, and individual roles, demanding a comprehensive and strategic approach to ensure successful adoption and integration.

This endeavor is not without challenge. I could almost feel the weight of it riding on his shoulders.

The room falls into a comfortable silence, allowing Dave to gather his thoughts and articulate his concerns. I am a trusted ally, ready to lend a listening ear and offer support whenever possible. Patiently, I wait for him to share his goals and challenges.

At the forefront of his concerns is stakeholder engagement, a task that encompasses a lengthy list of individuals with diverse needs and expectations. Dave is acutely aware of the importance of effectively communicating the reasons behind the changes and addressing the inevitable questions that will arise. However, the flow of information from the consulting firm guiding the project adds an element of unpredictability, leaving Dave to grapple with the uncertainty of having all the answers himself. As he gazes out the window, his mind drifts to imaginary encounters with stakeholders, each presenting unique challenges and requiring delicate navigation.

Staffing poses another hurdle for Dave to overcome. With his team already stretched thin, he needs people to provide training to different departments, so users know how to use the new system. Scheduling and ensuring adequate training for each department becomes a crucial responsibility for Dave's team, who must ensure the successful adoption and utilization of the new products throughout the organization.

The weight of expectations from senior leadership weighs

heavily on Dave's shoulders. His supervisor, nearing retirement, views this implementation as his legacy, the pinnacle of his thirty-year tenure. The executive team also hopes to showcase their ability to drive change. Dave's posture slouches as he speaks, perhaps reflecting his immense responsibility.

In addition to these demands, Dave was thrust into a pivotal role within the National Transition Team, responsible for implementing the transformation across all locations. This task demonstrates their technological expertise on a national scale and provides visibility for the entire department. Dave questions whether he will have enough time to fulfill these expectations while ensuring a successful implementation. Balancing work commitments with his personal life becomes a juggling act for Dave, who struggles to find quality time with his family. The thought of potentially sacrificing a planned vacation with his loved ones looms over him, highlighting the sacrifices required by his role.

Despite his extensive experience, Dave recognized that he needed help. This project wasn't a one-person show but a collaborative effort that required a profound understanding of change dynamics. He and his team were trained in the change management process. Dave knew he had the technical expertise but also wanted help navigating the human side of change—the resistance, the fear of the unknown, and the inevitable disruptions to established routines. He reached out for support, hiring me and my company.

Dave's concerns were multifaceted. He grappled with questions like how to align departments with divergent priorities and whether employees would embrace or resist the implementation of new technologies. Dave understood that this endeavor would demand significant effort and additional hours from his team, potentially necessitating personal sacrifices.

Simultaneously, he saw the project as an opportunity to spotlight his team's exceptional abilities, aspiring for recognition from senior management. He was eager for his team to receive the exposure and credit they rightfully deserved from the upper echelons of the organization.

These very apprehensions prompted Dave to seek guidance. While he had previously led successful changes, he acknowledged that this transformation posed unique challenges. Dave recognized the need for a fresh perspective and a strategic approach to enhance both his and his team's capabilities. Building an effective communication plan that transcended departmental interests and fostered collaboration and coherence became a pressing necessity.

As Dave concluded his account, I leaned forward, meeting his gaze with a reassuring smile. I knew the journey ahead wouldn't be without its challenges, but I was also confident that Dave had the change-ready skills to lead his team through this transformation. In this moment and the ones to come, my role was to provide him with the tools, strategies, and insights to empower him to navigate this path with clarity, resilience, and purpose.

As we began this transformative journey together, it became evident that Changeability was to be Dave's compass. Initiating and driving change would mean shifting the mindset and the skills of others. He anticipated people might not like having how they manage their day-to-day operations changed, from how they scheduled their meetings to the way department leaders would secure the resources they needed. It wasn't just about embracing change; it was about helping others to see the change as positive for efficiency and the organization's growth. Through strategic guidance, skill amplification, and an unshakable commitment to his team's success, Dave navigated the complexities of digital transformation.

Using the Changeability Framework™, Dave and his team succeeded. What was the process?

We started by taking a baseline assessment. Assessment results indicated which skills to leverage and identify gaps we needed to fill through coaching and training. We discussed the mindset, mental flexibility, and grit required to achieve their goals. We had honest conversations about concerns. We developed a success plan customized to Dave's personality and approach.

Next, we focused on how to motivate others and reduce resistance. Dave built his communication plan through scripting and learning to manage differing perspectives, communicating the reasons behind the change, emphasizing the positive aspects, and highlighting how it aligns with the organization's goals and values. He learned new skills to build upon his ability to empathize with the concerns of individuals and proactively engage them in dialogue, fostering a sense of ownership and understanding. Discovering how to build a foundation of psychological safety, Dave created a work environment that encourages collaboration, risk-taking, and creativity. He actively involved team members in the change process, soliciting their input and empowering them to contribute their ideas and solutions, encouraging their team members to embrace change, view it as an opportunity for growth, and actively seek out new knowledge and skills. He created an environment where individuals felt empowered to adapt, take risks, and contribute to the organization's agility and resilience. This culture of Changeability supported the organization's ability to respond to and drive innovation through digital transformation effectively.

Once Dave aligned the goals and the action plan, we focused on stakeholder engagement. It is essential to recognize that different stakeholders may have varying perspectives, needs, and concerns regarding the change. As a result, Dave engaged stakeholders early on, building relationships and establishing open lines of communication. He showed empathy and actively listened to stakeholders' perspectives, seeking common ground, and addressing concerns. Dave learned how to adapt his communication styles to resonate with each stakeholder, fostering trust and building a shared commitment to the change initiative. He was able to engage all levels within the organization successfully. His change in leadership, promotion of adaptability within his team, and agility to quickly lead and deliver change became the hallmarks of his administration.

Change leadership, adaptability, and agility strengthened the organization's Changeability. Through coaching, consulting, and the framework of Changeability, Dave could address challenges by embracing change, navigating uncertainty, inspiring, and engaging others, effectively managing stakeholders, and fostering a change-ready culture. By embodying Changeability, he has become a powerful catalyst for driving successful change initiatives and creating positive and lasting impact within his organizations.

As the organization reaped the rewards of its successful transition, so did Dave. The relationships he had nurtured, and the visibility positioned him as a respected change leader within his organization and the industry. His journey exemplified the essence of Changeability—the ability to lead change by embracing one's innate capabilities and leveraging them to shape a brighter future.

What is Change Leadership?

As an experienced leader, you're probably familiar with change management. It involves following a predefined process or methodology to implement change. These change management processes are essential in guiding transformation. However, the challenge lies in the fact that methods and models are constantly evolving. There are various approaches available, such as Kotter's 8-Step Change Model, McKinsey's 7-S framework, Agile Change Management, Prosci's ADKAR model (Awareness, Desire, Knowledge, Ability, and Reinforcement), The Disney Way, GE's change model, and many others. Regardless of the specific process chosen, change leadership is the driving force behind it all.

Change leadership, in the context of changeability, refers to the proactive and strategic process of guiding and influencing individuals, teams, and organizations through transitions and transformations. It involves setting a clear vision for change, effectively communicating that vision, and mobilizing people to embrace and drive change initiatives. Change leadership within the framework of changeability focuses on cultivating the mindset, skills, and behaviors necessary to initiate, lead, and navigate change with agility and resilience, ultimately driving positive outcomes and fostering a culture of adaptability.

In other words, change management serves as the vehicle for implementing change, while change leadership is the driver that steers the process toward success. Your leadership qualities, strategies, and skills genuinely make the difference in the success of any change initiative, regardless of the specific change management model or methodology you choose to follow.

Change leadership is at the foundational heart of Changeability—the guiding force that inspires, motivates, and drives successful change initiatives.

Change leadership is about more than just implementing new strategies or driving organizational shifts. It goes beyond that. It is about understanding the intricacies of human behavior, influencing mindsets, and creating a culture that embraces change as an opportunity for growth and innovation.

As a change catalyst, you can shape your organization's future, guide your team through uncertain times, and unleash their full potential. You are responsible for leading employees and teams through the transition process, ensuring they can successfully adapt to and leverage the benefits of the implemented changes.

By focusing on leadership, fostering adaptability, and embracing agility, you can create a powerful combination that drives meaningful organizational change. With these components working harmoniously, you are better equipped to navigate the complexities of change, gain buy-in from stakeholders, foster accountability within teams, and engage critical stakeholders effectively.

Think of change management as the vehicle, while change leadership is the driver. The leadership qualities, strategies, and skills you bring to the table determine the success of any change initiative, regardless of the specific change management model or methodology you adopt.

Dave highlighted that change leadership has challenges, even for the most experienced and seasoned change leaders. The change goes beyond simply following a model or methodology to manage the process. It demands clear and customized communication tailored to each stakeholder, as well as the presence of confident leaders who remain steadfast and unwavering in the face of difficulties. It requires a focused and determined approach, with the firm belief that regardless of the obstacles encountered, success is achievable, and the benefits of that success will make a significant impact.

Yet leading change can be tiring. Whether it is a new

product launch, a digital transformation, adapting to the use of leveraging artificial intelligence or any of the thousands of other changes leaders like yourself encounter, change leadership takes fortitude, skill and relentless dedication.

However, it is not a surprise that change isn't always successful.

Why Change Fails

"All organizations have warts," Nancy said on today's Zoom call. "It doesn't matter if you have twenty-two, two hundred, or two thousand people; the source of the problem is a people problem." Nancy, a Chief Human Resources Officer, downsized from working in a global manufacturing company to join a semiconductor non-profit organization with twenty-two employees. She began to list a litany of problems she encounters daily. I leaned forward as she documented the alphabet of concerns, all starting with the letter "P." She folded her arms across her chest as if protecting herself from the elements as she listed them. "All businesses have people, process, and product problems which ultimately create profit problems."

Of the "P's" people, process, product, profit, and I would add another "P," politics; which of these is the foremost concern in your organization?

Each can erode the future of any organization. The impact of these concerns exacerbates in times of change. The failure rate of change initiatives has been a topic of interest for many researchers and practitioners. While the exact failure rate can vary depending on the study and the definition of "failure," it is widely accepted that many change initiatives fail. The failure rate is estimated to be as high as seventy percent according to McKinsey research or within the range of fifty to seventy percent (based on studies by Harvard Business Review, Bain & Company, and various other consulting firms).

What gets in the way of success? There are several reasons, such as:

- Resistance to Change: One of the most common challenges is resistance from individuals or groups affected by the change. People may be resistant due to fear, uncertainty, or a perceived threat to their status quo. Overcoming resistance and gaining buy-in is crucial for successful change implementation. Realize that resistance is a normal reaction and develop the skills, like Dave, to align for change.

- Lack of Vision and Clarity: With a clear vision and well-defined goals, change efforts can become cohesive and maintain direction. Articulate a compelling vision that inspires and motivates others to embrace change.

- Communication Breakdown: Effective communication is essential during change, but ensuring all stakeholders understand and receive messages can be challenging. Miscommunication or adequate communication channels can lead to clarity, rumors, and resistance. Discover the differing perspectives people might have about change and adapt your communication. Establish open lines of communication and address any misunderstandings promptly.

- Organizational Culture: Change can be disruptive to established organizational cultures and norms. Overcoming resistance from deeply ingrained cultural beliefs and practices requires understanding the existing culture and strategically aligning the change efforts with the desired cultural values.

- Resource Constraints: Change initiatives often require additional financial, human, and technological resources. Limited resources can pose a significant challenge: finding creative solutions and prioritizing resources to support the change process effectively.

- Leadership Alignment: When multiple leaders are involved in driving change, differences in politics, perspectives, priorities, or approaches can hinder progress. Work collaboratively, align your strategies, and ensure a unified leadership front to overcome conflicts or disagreements.

- Change Fatigue: If an organization or individuals experience frequent or prolonged periods of change, they may become fatigued and resistant to further changes. Consider the pace and timing of change initiatives to avoid overwhelming stakeholders and maintain their engagement and commitment.

- Measurement and Evaluation: Assessing the impact and effectiveness of change efforts can be challenging. Establish appropriate metrics and evaluation processes to track progress, identify areas for improvement, and demonstrate the value of the change to stakeholders.

What changes are you currently facing? Are any of these concerns slowing you down? Failure means the organization and its customers fail to benefit from the change initiative, adequate profitability, competitive potential, and even the engagement and motivation of your employees. It can also reflect on your team. My goal is to empower every leader to succeed.

When I partner with leaders and their teams, I can see their potential and I also see the root cause of any symptoms. What is most frustrating for my clients is slow momentum, wasted time and re-work. Failure to make quick decisions, engage cross functional teams and prioritize the stream of work only adds stress.

By anticipating and addressing these challenges by unleashing your and your team's Changeability you will navigate change successfully, preserve your sanity, and deliver desired outcomes.

And, like Dave, you can tap into your own team's creative potential.

Overcoming the Barriers to Change Leadership

You have likely established a solid process for change management. However, it is crucial to recognize that managing the "people side" of change involves navigating the intricate realm of human dynamics. This messy stuff can make or break a change initiative.

Some of the concerns expressed by our clients are as follows. Are you currently experiencing any of these issues?

Stagnant Innovation: They notice a need for fresh ideas, creative problem-solving, and a reluctance to embrace change. They seek assistance in igniting innovation and creating a culture that fosters continuous improvement and adaptation.

Resistance to Change: They observe employees needing to be more open to new initiatives, exhibiting low morale, and struggling to navigate through transitions. They understand the need for changeability coaching to address resistance, improve change readiness, and create a smoother change management process.

Declining Competitiveness: Clients may identify a decline in their organization's competitiveness and market position. Their competitors are outpacing them in innovation, adaptability, and customer-centric approaches. They want to revitalize their organization, leveraging Changeability coaching to enhance their competitive advantage, regain market share, and stay relevant in a rapidly changing business landscape.

Lack of Employee Engagement: A department or organizational assessment indicates decreased employee engagement and satisfaction. Leaders observe disengaged employees, reduced collaboration, and a need for more ownership in driving innovation and change.

Building the Capacity for Change: They are frustrated and tired of repeating themselves as people question the goal and worry about the lack of accountability. They want to sharpen their leadership skills to build effective communication, conflict management, influence, and negotiation skills. Or they might feel overwhelmed and burnt out and desire the skills to strive and to have a champion in their corner.

Develop a Pipeline of Future Ready Leaders: Future-ready leaders have discovered, activated, or amplified the skillset of Changeability, leading change regardless of position, having a mindset, skillset, and toolset of adaptability, and responding to change quickly. Leaders and teams cultivate a growth mindset and view change as an opportunity versus an obstacle.

Clients reach out because while the symptoms are recognizable, they aren't sure of the root cause and want a diagnosis and an actionable plan. I identify the root cause through a combination of science-based assessments, gained insights, and the extensive experience of collaborating with numerous teams. In Chapter 9 you will discover how a team experienced innovation, growth while delivering business results through this process. Despite any people, process, product, or profitability challenges, you likely have a talented team. You have what it takes to win the race, it's eliminating obstacles and unleashing your team's full potential that will give you the lift you might desire.

While I can't provide all possible solutions in a book, I can offer strategies for tackling the most common challenges.

Strategies for Tackling the Tough Challenges

Politics: Aligning Your Priority to What Already Matters

Navigating internal politics can be painful if you are unaware of the invisible rules. Understanding hidden agendas, who the key decision-makers are, and learning how to influence them will help you succeed.

While internal politics can be daunting, it is crucial to driving organizational change. To effectively tackle this challenge, aligning your priorities with what already matters to key decision-makers is essential.

First, identify the individuals with the political currency relevant to your current goals. Write their name and their role in a document.

Once you have identified these key decision-makers, understand their motivations and interests. What do they care about the most? What aspects of the organization or their roles hold significant importance to them?

Next, consider the priorities that these decision-makers are responsible for executing. What goals are they pursuing, and how is their success measured within the organization? By aligning your initiatives with their objectives, you can highlight the relevance and value of your proposed changes. Consider how your topic intersects with their priorities and articulate the potential benefits and positive impact it can have on their areas of responsibility. Demonstrating the alignment between your goals and theirs can increase your chances of gaining their support and buy-in.

You have documented their name, role, priorities, and shared goals to build your stakeholder engagement strategy. Write down your objective; what do you want to accomplish through this relationship? From there, develop your communication plan. How might you adapt your communication to each individual?

Politics within an organization can be complex, but by strategically aligning your priorities with key decision-makers, you can navigate this landscape more effectively. When understanding their motivations, communication preferences, and priorities, you can craft a compelling case highlighting your proposed changes' mutual benefits.

To illustrate the impact of aligning priorities, consider a client's real-life example.

Strategic Alignment: Business Objectives and Senior Leadership Priorities

For over two years, a clinical care director tirelessly pursued funding for a technology solution aimed at enhancing information sharing among physicians, with the goal of improving overall efficiency. Despite her passionate advocacy and numerous attempts, securing approval for the necessary technology and resources proved elusive. The primary challenges were the project's cost, which exceeded the allocated budget, and the substantial investment required. Each presentation she made to senior leadership received a respectful hearing, yet none led to project approval.

The organization sought my assistance following a recent merger, which, while well-planned, had not yielded the anticipated financial benefits due to cultural clashes between the two previously separate entities. In the process of designing the merged culture, I had an opportunity to support the Director.

Senior leadership's focus lay on cost reduction, efficiency enhancement, and enhancing patient access and satisfaction scores.

In a large conference room, the Director and I sat together, her persistent concern being her inability to gain approval for her proposal. I proposed aligning her initiative with the organization's priorities as a solution. Collaboratively, we crafted an exhaustive communication plan and formulated a robust business case.

Our initial step involved evaluating the current process and its impact on the organization. Research revealed that the existing process required over ten days to complete, while the proposed technological solution offered by my client could reduce this time to less than two days. Subsequently, we assessed how process improvement would align with the organization's existing objectives, taking into account the CEO and CFO's primary emphasis on achieving measurable enhancements in patient access and satisfaction.

With this understanding, the director built her business

case. Despite her previous rejections, she hesitantly accepted the challenge. Side by side, we meticulously reviewed every aspect, examining metrics and the return on investment. Consequently, she revamped her proposal, emphasizing the adverse effects of the current processes on doctors' availability for patient care, resulting in reduced patient access. The proposal was submitted to the CEO and CFO, and she presented it at the Monday morning meeting. Thanks to our thorough preparation, she felt well-prepared, and her confidence in this opportunity was palpable.

Previously perceived as just another individual seeking funds from a resource-constrained organization, the management team now regarded the clinical director as a leader who understood how to leverage data and metrics to present a business case for positive change. This change would address a problem that was already a priority within the organization. The director's diligence paid off as her solution resonated with the CEO and CFO, aligning with their core priorities of increased access to doctors and improved patient satisfaction scores.

Consequently, the director's request gained the attention it deserved, and the necessary funding was approved. Ultimately, she achieved the outcome she had tirelessly pursued. This example underscores the effectiveness of aligning priorities when navigating organizational politics and priorities. By comprehending key decision-makers' concerns and motivations and framing proposals to address their pressing needs, you can successfully garner support for change initiatives, even in the face of initial resistance.

She was able to bridge the gap by aligning her objectives with her organization's priorities.

Communication: Meet them at the intersection of WIIFM

When I work from home, one of my three golden retrievers, Jack Petty (named after Tom Petty of Tom Petty and The Heartbreakers), sometimes barks for no apparent reason. I often find myself asking him, "What do you want?" Is it a lost ball under the couch, the need to go outside, or simply boredom from watching me in my office all day? Most of the time, I can't quite figure it out. Communication works similarly.

By paying close attention to people's words, you can discern their top priorities and position yourself at the intersection of your objectives and their "what's in it for me" (WIIFM) mindset. I assist leaders in tailoring their communication with others by analyzing and identifying the recipient's potential needs or preferences.

Many years ago, I read an article by John Nicolls in the *Leadership and Organizational Development Journal* titled "Head, Heart, and Hands: Transforming Leadership."

Nicolls defined strategic leadership as the "head" aspect, focusing on vision, goals, and mission. Supervisory leadership relates to managing people to perform tasks, the "hands." Transformational leadership encompasses the "heart," establishing a genuine human connection with others. I also found this concept of head, heart, and hands applicable to communication. I noticed that the words people use help to profile what they care about most: the goal, the impact on people, the process, or the execution—head, heart, or hands. In 2014, I became certified in a change leadership assessment tool that follows a similar strategy. It helps individuals identify their change leadership preference (head, heart, or hands) and their team's. All three are needed. However, many teams either miss key components or are too heavily weighted in one area. Imagine being all goal and execution focused without considering the impact on people. Or being so people-focused that a team fails to develop an action plan. Many change leaders are hands-focused, utilizing a process and roadmap to deliver on their goals. Adding heart-felt connection and communication allows them to get buy-in much faster. Healthcare tends to be very heart-centered yet needs people on the team to provide strategy and a process to achieve its goals. Executives tend to focus on overarching goals and use their teams to put their hands to work to make their vision a reality. Marketing and communications often focus on the heart side of communication: how will words impact people's emotions?

So, how can you use your head, heart, and hands to improve communication?

You can begin by adapting your communication by aligning with the other person's head, heart, or hands focus. First, pay attention to the words they use. Those who emphasize the "head" often talk about goals and results. Those prioritizing the "hands" tend to discuss processes, roadmaps, required resources, and practical execution. In contrast, those who resonate with the "heart" focus on people, team members, and customers. They consider how individuals will be affected by the change and strive for positive outcomes for everyone involved. Begin your conversation with their preference, head, heart or hands. Examples might include "You want the department to meet its fifteen percent contribution to overhead." Or "The team is feeling overwhelmed with the number of projects," or "Our roadmap is right on schedule; meeting with the customer is our next action."

Now, let's take a moment to reflect on yourself and your

team members individually. Grab a piece of paper and write "Head," "Heart," and "Hands" across the top. List the names of your team members on the left side. Think of your last team meeting; what was their focus? Do they lean more toward the head, heart, or hands? Note these observations on the paper. Additionally, consider your communication style during times of change.

With this insight, you can tailor your conversations to align with others' priorities by identifying whether they lean toward the head, heart, or hands. Remember, individuals may emphasize one aspect more frequently than the others or transition between them. The key is initiating conversations in their respective focus zone, centered around their "What's in it for me" (WIIFM) perspective. This approach will enable you to engage and involve people more effectively, fostering faster and more aligned progress. Teams work together more collaboratively and cohesively, making quicker decisions and reducing friction.

You can use the same method with your senior leaders' leaders, collaborating departments, and with your stakeholders. By understanding how to use the Head, Heart, and Hands communication, you can connect with individuals' values and aspirations and create alignment more readily.

Building Lasting Relationships with Stakeholders

Stakeholder engagement and relationship building are essential cornerstones for effective change leadership. In today's business environment, change leaders play a pivotal role in guiding their teams and organizations towards successful transitions.

To navigate these changes successfully, change leaders must recognize that their efforts extend beyond strategic planning and implementation. They must also cultivate strong relationships with various stakeholders, both internal and external, to garner support, build consensus, and drive sustainable change. These stakeholders may include employees, peers, senior leaders, customers, suppliers, and even regulatory bodies.

The ability to engage and connect with these stakeholders can make the difference between a change initiative's success or failure. In this context, change leaders must wear multiple hats: communicator, motivator, influencer, and collaborator. They must be adept at understanding the unique perspectives, concerns, and motivations of each stakeholder group and tailor their approach accordingly.

Let's explore strategies, techniques, and best practices to effectively navigate the intricate web of relationships. Managing stakeholder relationships is a significant challenge for many clients. Achieving alignment among different departments, teams, and stakeholders requires effective communication, collaboration, and breaking down silos. Recognizing this frustration, I developed a program to enhance stakeholder engagement. To get you started some of the action items are listed below.

To excel in stakeholder engagement and effective communication, it's crucial to follow a strategic approach. Start by identifying the specific priorities of your individual stakeholders or departments. This step is vital because stakeholders often have diverse interests, concerns, and perspectives. Avoid the common mistake of assuming that all stakeholders share similar goals.

For instance, consider Dave's experience, who initially feared navigating the complex landscape of various stakeholders. Once he understood the importance of tailoring his communication to each stakeholder's priorities, he became much more effective. Dave realized that stakeholders could range from skeptics and inquisitors to big-picture thinkers and detail-oriented individuals. Instead of delivering a one-size-fits-all message, Dave learned to flex his communication style, adopting head, heart, and hands perspectives. This adaptability made him appear confident, professional, and capable in the eyes of others.

In addition to verbal communication, pay attention to non-verbal cues such as body language, facial expressions, and tone of voice. These cues can provide valuable insights into a stakeholder's engagement level or concerns. If you notice any signs of disengagement or hesitancy, address them directly by asking open-ended questions like, "Is there something I missed?" or "Might you have some concerns about this idea?" This approach fosters better communication and collaboration with stakeholders.

If you find reaching out to stakeholders with different interests or values uncomfortable, there's a solution for you as well. Building professional relationships doesn't require socializing or becoming personal friends. Instead, focus on three primary objectives: visibility, branding, and collaboration.

Visibility: Building relationships helps establish recognition within your organization both vertically and horizontally, enabling you to build a robust network of relationships.

Branding: Your relationships can speak volumes about your professional brand. While many individuals may feel uncomfortable showcasing their results, increased visibility through relationships highlights your capabilities and those of your team.

Collaboration: Ultimately, the goal of relationship building is to work together effectively on tasks and projects.

By aligning your efforts with these objectives, you can approach stakeholder engagement with a clear purpose. Remember that the primary goal is to achieve results and foster productive working relationships rather than necessarily having a personal affinity for every stakeholder.

Strategies for Boosting Team Engagement and Accountability

You have a great team, but you may worry now and then about performance. There are several ways to boost team engagement and accountability.

Establish a shared vision and clear goals. Describe your plan for the project and ask your team to contribute by asking, "What else is possible?" A team takes greater ownership of the outcome when they help to create the goals. With a clear target, it is easier for your team to understand the meaning of a project or why it matters.

Identify your non-negotiables: with the team, identify teaming agreements. A teaming agreement is how the team will work best together through this project. You can also do this with cross-functional departments. What are our mutual expectations? What will we not tolerate? What can we commit to holding each other accountable for? Examples my clients have used for non-negotiables are mutual respect, idea sharing, listening before responding, keeping each other informed and no hiding on accountability, no backstabbing, and no delayed feedback.

Know and Grow Your Team: Know people as individuals and identify ways to grow them. Once you understand the strengths of each team member, you can delegate tasks you have done yourself. For example, look at your calendar. Which individuals on your team are ready to participate in the meetings you now attend? Some of my clients feel guilty or worry that they are "dumping" work on the team when I discuss this topic. No, when you enable individuals to attend meetings on your behalf, you benefit them. They gain exposure to different organizational levels, learn more about their department's priorities, and gain personal visibility for their career trajectory. Your delegation grows them.

Next, look at the presentations or reports you deliver. Who might develop a skeleton draft for you or provide the entire report? How can you grow your team by giving them opportunities to have new experiences within the organization? How can they grow by embracing a stretch goal? The 90-Day Action Focus Teams I lead accomplish more in ninety days than the organization ever imagined. Why? Because participants had a safe space to problem solve, innovate, learn, and try on new skills and, in essence, stretch and grow. When given these opportunities you are not only developing their change leadership, but you also promote adaptability, creativity and create a safe space for exploration and innovation. Plus, you gain back time to focus on what is most important.

I coached an overwhelmed senior manager facing an endless list of projects to delegate more to his team. He normally would have spent endless weeks either doing the projects himself or micromanaging their tasks. Instead, he announced at the team meeting "These are the projects we need to accomplish in two months; how will we get it done?" Soon, all managers selected a task to accomplish. The work was completed in two months, in less time than expected. He found that shifting from micromanaging and doing it "all" himself to delegating, engaging, and coaching his management team freed him up to think more strategically and focus more on what mattered the most. He used this time to expand services within a client organization, to develop relationships within several departments and to gain visibility for himself and his team.

Create a Culture of Ownership and Accountability: Develop a shared sense of accountability for outcomes and results and encourage team members to take ownership of their work and responsibilities. To spur ownership, ask versus assign. Communicate the task: "We need to build a custom part for Boeing and get it to California within two days. How can we get it done?"

Building accountability within your team is your gateway to freedom. Imagine having more time, time to get to the gym after work, to focus on a critical initiative, to spend time with your loved ones or to relax without worrying about work.

If you find your team less than accountable, use this "Debora-ism," a name a CEO coined for the mini frameworks I offer to my clients. To build accountability, end every meeting and every conversation with "Who will do what by when, and how will I know?" This sentence provides clarity and commitment and builds a common language for accountability. Imagine leaving every meeting clear on roles, responsibilities, and obligations. Envision your team members reporting the status of every project with a clear trajectory of timeframe and commitment. No more wondering who took on the tasks assigned from the meeting or when individuals will complete their work. No need to micromanage or lay awake at night looking at the ceiling with worry.

When my clients put these strategies in place, they are free to strive for even more excellent opportunities while having time to enjoy the rewards of their success. They dance on the Caribbean beaches, take extended vacations, and enjoy their lives. They expand their business nationwide into new markets, overtake their competitors, and equally, if not more importantly, work and life become more enjoyable. While my company measures many metrics, it is when I see my clients enjoying their work and their lives that I know I've succeeded.

Which of these strategies might make leadership easier for you? Which is easy enough for you to put into practice tomorrow?

Forward Actions:

1. Take the Change Leadership Assessment: Consider taking the Change Leadership assessment to identify your leadership style. Determine whether you lean more toward leading with your head (goal-oriented), heart (people-oriented), or hands (execution-oriented). Understanding your leadership style can help you leverage your strengths and adapt to different styles.

2. Reflect on Your Leadership Journey: Take time to reflect on your leadership journey so far. What have been your most significant successes and challenges in leading change? Reflecting on your experiences can provide valuable insights for future growth. Share your learnings with your team to help them grow.

3. Set Personal Development Goals: Consider developing your internal power base. What relationship would help to support your personal and professional goals? What stakeholder relationships might you want to nurture? Seek out one competency to develop. Whether it's improving communication, enhancing empathy, refining strategic planning, delegating so you can prioritize your time, or developing your team.

4. Seek Feedback: Request feedback from your team members, peers, or mentors regarding your change leadership style. Constructive feedback can offer a fresh perspective on your strengths and areas for improvement, helping you refine your approach.
5. Stay Updated: Stay informed about the latest trends in your business and industry. This will promote your visibility and thought leadership.

By taking these forward actions, you can continue to evolve as a change leader, effectively guiding your team through the challenges and opportunities that change brings.

Now, as we transition into the next chapter on adaptability, remember that leadership in change goes hand in hand with the ability to adapt. A strong leader not only initiates change but also embodies the adaptability needed to navigate it successfully. So, as you venture into the realm of adaptability, keep in mind that it's not just about responding to change—it's about doing so with agility, resilience, and a forward-thinking mindset.

CHAPTER 4

Adaptability: Empowering Your Team for Digital Transformation and Innovation

> *"The ability to adapt and learn, to take risks and turn ideas into action, is essential for success in the changing workplace."*
>
> —**Korn Ferry**

"It doesn't work," my client said. "We follow the change management process, but it doesn't work. People don't listen, they are slow to adapt, and we will miss our delivery date for the project; what can I do?"

Shahana, a leader known for her adeptness in managing complex projects, faced a formidable challenge. A critical project from a valued customer had landed on her desk, accompanied by an imposing deadline. It wasn't unusual for her company to customize solutions for their largest customers, a trait that made them a desirable vendor partner but also burdened the staff with constant change.

The successful completion of this project was non-negotiable, and Shahana recognized that significant changes within her team's processes and approach were essential to meet the customer's demands.

With her characteristic professionalism and determination, Shahana introduced the necessary changes requested by the customer to her team. She explained the benefits of adopting a more streamlined and efficient methodology, emphasizing how this shift would not only ensure success for the current project but also enhance overall team performance and foster professional growth.

To Shahana's surprise, despite her efforts to rationalize the benefits and provide support, the team members remained reluctant to embrace the new approach.

As the project progressed, it became evident that the team's resistance to change was causing significant delays. The existing processes were ill-suited for the project's requirements, leading to difficulties meeting the customer's deadline. Frustration mounted as the project's progress stagnated, threatening the team's reputation and customer satisfaction.

Shahana confided in me that she needed help in rallying

the team. Recognizing the situation's urgency, I introduced the concepts of adaptability, emphasizing the importance of mindset and mental flexibility. It became apparent that understanding the team's perspective and encouraging them to view the project from the customer's standpoint was pivotal in transforming resistance into resilience.

Through a few laser-focused meetings, Shahana quickly learned and applied the skills provided.

Gradually, Shahana's persistent efforts began yielding results. The team members started grasping the importance of adapting their processes to meet the project's demands. With renewed enthusiasm and a shared commitment, they worked together to gain traction to meet the customer's deadline quickly.

Shahana guided the project's remaining phases, offering mentorship and support as needed. Despite initial setbacks, the team rallied and successfully delivered the project, a testament to their resilience and newfound adaptability.

Have you ever found yourself in a scenario where your team resisted crucial changes, even in the face of impending deadlines or heightened customer expectations? This common challenge often underscores the importance of adaptability within teams and organizations. Whether it's embracing new methodologies, accommodating shifting market demands, or addressing customer requirements, adaptability is the key to not just surviving but thriving.

What is Adaptability?

Focus on an experience where you experienced a significant disruption in your work environment. On a scale of one to five, how would you rate your readiness to adapt in the face of that change?

Thinking about that change, what was difficult about it? What was easy? What would you have kept the same? What might you have done differently?

Adaptability is about having a positive relationship with change. Most barriers to change are people related. There is a fear of the unknown. Team members lack the skills they need during times of change. There is miscommunication, or resistance to change.

Adaptability is the 2nd pillar of the Changeability triangle. Adaptability strengthens you and your team's ability to navigate change, and the third pillar, agility, speeds delivery.

Adaptability is the ability to adjust, innovate, and embrace change with agility and resilience. It refers to the ability of individuals, teams, and organizations to adjust to new or changing circumstances, environments, requirements, or situations. An adaptable team exhibits flexibility, versatility, and responsiveness, coupled with a willingness and ability to learn, grow, and improve. They can quickly assess situations, identify necessary changes, and take appropriate actions to achieve their goals, even in the face of uncertainty or adversity. It allows them to swiftly refocus their efforts, adjust their strategies, and embrace new technologies or processes to maintain a competitive edge and achieve success. Moreover, adaptability breeds resilience, enabling teams to navigate unexpected challenges with agility and creativity.

Take a moment to think about the last change implemented. Were there times when you wondered how the most meticulously crafted plan could be delayed, or worse veer off course? Often it isn't because of your change in leadership, it is attributed to the strength of your team's adaptability. Your team might have the skills to adapt however as noted earlier, they may be latent, inactivated or unleveraged.

Lack of adaptability manifests itself in various ways. For instance, team members may exhibit resistance or rejection of new ideas, processes, or technologies introduced to enhance efficiency and effectiveness. Instead of embracing change, they cling to familiar routines and methods, inadvertently creating a stagnant environment that hampers growth and stifles innovation.

Additionally, individuals who lack adaptability may struggle to respond to unexpected challenges or setbacks. They may become overwhelmed, resistant to change, or easily discouraged when confronted with unfamiliar situations or shifting priorities. This rigidity can impede problem-solving and hinder the team's ability to overcome obstacles and achieve its goals.

Diminished adaptability can be incredibly frustrating. It creates roadblocks to progress and dampens your team's potential. You rely on your team members to be flexible, open-minded, and eager to learn and grow. When team members resist change or struggle to adapt, it generates tension, slows decision-making processes, and ultimately hinders the team's ability to seize opportunities that lie before them.

Moreover, a lack of adaptability can have far-reaching implications for the organization. Adaptability is crucial for maintaining competitiveness in today's rapidly evolving business landscape. As a leader, you need your team to be responsive to market trends, customer needs, and technological advancements. Without adaptability, your team risks falling behind competitors, missing out on growth opportunities, and struggling to navigate the ever-changing business landscape.

But here's the good news: adapting is a learnable skill, and it can be cultivated through coaching and skill-building initiatives. By building your team's adaptability, you can empower them to embrace change, think outside the box, and confidently tackle uncertainties.

Adaptability as a Game Changer

Adaptability is used to improve and support employee wellbeing, change and transformation, innovation, company culture, leadership development and talent retention.

Once you know how to leverage and equip your team with the necessary tools, they will adapt to change with speed and agility. You will unleash skills such as a growth mindset, promote continuous learning, and encourage individuals to embrace new ideas and approaches. With time and practice, your team will develop the resilience and agility required to adapt to any circumstance that comes their way.

When you are adaptable, you are not limited by rigid thinking or resistance to change. You don't panic like the man needing a pen. As new technologies evolve, you embrace them and evolve, too. It's an attitude shift; you embrace change as an invitation to grow and evolve, recognizing that the status quo is not a fixed destination but a starting point for exploration. By being open to new ideas, perspectives, and ways of doing things, you and your team can unlock the potential for innovation and creativity.

As a result, adaptability empowers you and your team to navigate uncharted territories with confidence and resilience. It equips you to quickly adjust your course, pivot your strategies, and find alternative solutions when unexpected obstacles arise. It allows you to remain agile in uncertainty and ambiguity, enabling you to turn challenges into opportunities.

Moreover, adaptability expands your capacity to learn and develop. It encourages your team to step outside their comfort zone, embrace new experiences, and acquire new skills.

Each adaptation will broaden their knowledge and expertise, becoming more versatile and prepared for whatever the future holds.

Building an adaptable team prevents the frustration Shahana experienced. There is no need to micromanage or worry if your team will achieve its goals.

Imagine the possibility of having a team that embraces change and eagerly embraces it, with a sense of curiosity and a desire to learn and grow. Picture a team that sees obstacles as opportunities and navigates through them with grace and determination.

Remember, the ability to adapt is not a fixed trait reserved for a select few; it's a skill that can be nurtured and honed. By building your team's adaptability, you are investing in their future success and the long-term prosperity of your organization.

An adaptable person or team can quickly assess a situation, identify the necessary changes, and take appropriate actions to achieve their goals, even amid uncertainty, ambiguity, or adversity. Moreover, adaptability breeds resilience, enabling teams to navigate unexpected challenges with agility and creativity.

The Top Skill Needed for the Future of Work

Adaptability is becoming a critical skill for employability.

- The World Economic Forum reports indicate that forty percent of today's jobs will not exist in ten years. Seventy percent of executives expressed the desire to increase their organization's ability to flex to change and cite that adaptability is their number one sought-after workforce capability.

- The LinkedIn Workforce Survey revealed adaptability as the most sought-after skill, rising from being a top-five skill in earlier years.

- Fifty-four percent of executives in a recent Deloitte global survey selected adaptability as one of the top three most critical workforce traits, more than technological savvy and alignment of values—and more than double the importance of critical thinking, creativity, empathy, and curiosity.

With the increase in the speed of change and the influx of AI solutions, all are challenged to adapt to new experiences. Adapting to new technologies, shifting market demands, and changing customer preferences is no longer optional—it is essential for survival. Those who fail to adapt to risk becoming obsolete, while those who embrace change can position themselves for success.

Adaptability enables organizations to respond swiftly to market dynamics, seize new opportunities, and effectively navigate challenges. It empowers individuals to acquire new skills, expand their knowledge, and embrace new ways of thinking. Organizations can foster innovation, agility, and resilience by cultivating a culture of adaptability.

Embracing change and adapting to new realities also opens doors to new possibilities. It allows organizations to uncover untapped markets, develop innovative products and services, and attract top talent. Individuals who embrace adaptability gain a competitive edge, opening up new career paths and opportunities for personal growth.

Resilience has been a recent focus. Resilience is about

bouncing back. Adaptability is about *leaping forward.* If resilience is the car, adaptability is the highway.

How adaptable is your team when it comes to change?

Many leaders are not sure how to respond. Adaptability wasn't something that was identifiable and measurable.

Until now.

AQ®, Adaptability and YOU: Adaptability Intelligence

As a coach/consultant specializing in guiding leaders through change, I constantly search for solutions that provide actionable insight and quick wins for my clients. I was immediately drawn to the Adaptability Quotient (AQ®) assessment developed by Adaptai Ltd, and underwent its intensive two-year training process to become a partner consultant.

What sets this assessment apart is its ability to provide unique insights not easily obtained through traditional employee engagement surveys or pulse assessments. It offers a deepened insight into the current state of adaptability and change readiness, offering invaluable information for transformation.

For the first time, adaptability is measurable at the individual, team, and organizational levels. Note, information doesn't lead to transformation without the insight mapping and bridge building to maximize the thinking and behaviors needed to produce business results.

You might be familiar with Emotional Intelligence, Adaptability Intelligence, developed by AQai®, also known as AQ® (Adaptability Quotient), refers to the capacity of individuals and organizations to effectively navigate and respond to changes in their environment.

Based on principles of psychology, a literary review of over 100 studies, and assessments of results from countries worldwide, the platform of adaptability developed, and the AQ® assessment was born. Correlations emerged, and the data generated guides the opportunity to help leaders, teams, and organizations thrive during change by gaining awareness and improving the critical pillars of adaptability. It encompasses three key areas that contribute to adaptability: Ability, Character, and Environment; the ability to adapt; the characteristics of those who adapt; and the environment in which adaptability takes place. Ability, Character, and Environment form the A.C.E. model. Ability provides insight into "How and to what degree do I adapt?" Character identifies "Who adapts and Why?" Environment specifies, "When does someone adapt and why?" Each area in the A.C.E. Model has five sub-dimensions. This assessment measures adaptability at the individual, team, and organizational levels.

Ability: Ability measures how you adapt to change and to what degree you can adapt.

Subdimensions measured include Grit, Mental Flexibility, Mindset, Resilience, and Unlearn.

- Grit refers to an individual's perseverance in facing challenges and setbacks. It measures their ability to maintain focus, overcome obstacles, and stay committed to their goals despite difficulties. Do you and your team "push on through," or are you bogged down and overwhelmed with change?
- Mental Flexibility assesses an individual's openness to new ideas, perspectives, and approaches. It measures their ability to adapt their thinking and embrace alternative and even opposing viewpoints. Those with high mental flexibility can quickly adjust their mindset

and perspectives in response to changing circumstances, enabling them to navigate uncertainties and explore innovative solutions. You can build this approach by inviting differing ideas. Challenge your team to ask themselves, "What else is possible?" or "How would a start-up organization view this opportunity?"

- Mindset refers to an individual's underlying beliefs and attitudes about their abilities and the nature of change. The AQ® assessment evaluates whether individuals have a growth mindset. A growth mindset fosters a positive attitude towards change, as individuals see challenges as opportunities for growth rather than obstacles. Many organizations I work with support a growth mindset as a leadership competency, yet, until now, we have been unable to measure it. Does your organization understand the value of a growth mindset to secure its future?

- Resilience measures an individual's ability to bounce back from setbacks, adapt to adversity, and recover quickly from challenging situations. It encompasses emotional resilience, mental toughness, and the capacity to cope with stress. Resilient individuals are better equipped to face change uncertainties, maintain their emotional well-being, and focus on achieving desired outcomes. What degree of resilience do you see in your team?

- Unlearn: Unlearning refers to the willingness and ability to let go of old habits, beliefs, and assumptions that may hinder adaptability. It involves challenging preconceived notions, questioning established processes, and embracing new ways of thinking and working. Unlearning allows individuals to break free from rigid thinking patterns and embrace change with an open mind. Think of a time when you had to implement a new working process. Was there pushback, or did the team readily embrace the change?

Each of these sub-dimensions plays a critical role in an individual's or team's adaptability. The ability to adapt is learnable; it is a skill that can be quickly embraced and utilized.

Character: Character is more innate and is built on a foundation of personal life and learning experiences. The subdimensions of Character are learnable and, with insight, modified and developed. However, development may take longer than the Ability sub-dimensions.

The Character dimension measures who adapts and what about their Character helps them adjust. This aspect of the AQ® assessment examines the personal qualities and attributes that contribute to adaptability. By understanding these characteristics, individuals, teams, and organizations can cultivate and enhance the qualities that support adaptability. Sub-dimensions include Emotional Range, Extraversion, Hope, Motivation Style, and Thinking Style.

- Emotional Range refers to the breadth and intensity of an individual's emotional experiences and expressions. Do you find some people to be more reactive than others? In the context of adaptability, individuals with a more comprehensive emotional range can navigate change more effectively, as they are equipped to handle the emotions and uncertainties that arise during times of transition.

- Extraversion: Extraversion assesses an individual's inclination towards seeking external stimulation and engaging with others. It measures their preference for social interaction, assertiveness, and energy levels in social settings. Those with higher levels of extraversion may find it easier to adapt to change, as they are more likely to seek support and collaborate with others during times of transition. Neither introvert nor extrovert Character is right or wrong; both might react differently during change, and it is helpful to understand their differences.

- Hope is an individual's belief in their ability to create positive outcomes and their expectation that the future will improve. It measures their optimism, resilience, and proactive mindset. Individuals with higher levels of hope are more likely to approach change as an opportunity for growth and actively work towards achieving desired outcomes, even in the face of challenges. Is your team hopeful or doubtful when facing the most demanding challenges?

- Motivation Style assesses an individual's preferred approach to motivation and the factors that drive their behavior. Are they motivated to play to win or focused on playing to protect? Do they work carefully to protect what they have, or are they willing to explore and feel energized by taking risks and improving or exploring new alternatives? Understanding one's motivation style is vital for adaptability, as it influences the individual's drive to learn, embrace change, and persist in facing challenges.

- Thinking Style: Thinking Style examines an individual's cognitive preferences and tendencies in processing information and making decisions. It explores whether individuals lean towards big-picture thinking, are detailed thinkers, or a balance of both. Different thinking styles can influence adaptability by shaping how individuals approach problem-solving, consider multiple perspectives, and navigate complex situations.

Embracing emotional range, leveraging extraversion, nurturing hope, aligning motivation style, and embracing diverse thinking styles can all build a foundation of adaptability that supports successful change navigation.

Environment: How we think and behave is molded by our environment. Environment in the A.C.E. model measures "when someone adapts and to what degree" and measures the specific elements required within the work environment to thrive during times of change. The sub-dimensions include Company Support, Emotional Health, Team Support, Work Environment, and Work Stress. Below are the definitions of each; as you read, think of your team and the organization's environment. Where do strengths exist? Where are there areas for improvement?

- Company Support refers to employees' general perception of how their organization values their contribution and cares about their well-being. A supportive company environment makes individuals feel empowered and motivated to adapt to change effectively.
- Emotional Health: Emotional Health evaluates the psychological well-being of individuals within the work environment. Do they experience more positive moments while limiting the negative? Are they thriving

and striving at work or only surviving? A work environment that prioritizes emotional health fosters resilience, reduces burnout, and enables individuals to cope with the challenges that change brings.

- Team Support: Team Support examines the level of collaboration, communication, and cohesion within teams during periods of change. It measures whether team members support one another, share information openly, and work together to navigate the complexities of change. Strong team support promotes trust, unity, and shared accountability, enhancing the collective ability to adapt and thrive.

- Work Environment: Does your organization encourage self-disruption, allow experimentation, and create psychological safety for ideas to be respectfully heard and explored? A conducive work environment encourages collaboration, innovation, and open dialogue, facilitating adaptability and building a foundation for successful change.

- Work Stress evaluates the stress and pressure experienced by individuals within the work environment during times of change. It considers factors such as workload, time constraints, and the perceived demands of change initiatives. With the rise in the mental health crisis, increased work stress leads to burnout, erodes productivity, and can lead to attrition. Managing work stress is crucial for maintaining productivity, mental well-being, and the ability to adapt effectively. Are you having open conversations with your team about work stress and how to mitigate its impact?

Assessing Your Team's Adaptability

By assessing and understanding how these subdivisions contribute to adaptability, individuals, teams, and organizations can gain valuable insights into their strengths and areas for development. This knowledge allows for targeted efforts in cultivating and enhancing these qualities, ultimately fostering a culture of adaptability, and enabling individuals to thrive in the face of change.

Building the ability to adapt plays a critical role in an individual's or team's adaptability. Grit ensures persistence and determination during challenging times. Mental flexibility enables the exploration of new possibilities and the ability to adapt to different situations. Mindset shapes one's perspective on change, either fostering a growth mindset that welcomes opportunities or a fixed mindset that resists change. Resilience supports emotional well-being and the ability to bounce back from setbacks. Unlearning promotes continuous improvement and a willingness to embrace new ways of doing things.

Increasing the characteristics that support striving through change, embracing emotional range, leveraging extraversion, nurturing hope, aligning motivation style, and embracing diverse thinking styles can all contribute to building a foundation of adaptability that supports the successful navigation of change. Lastly, a supportive company culture emphasizing emotional health, strong team support, a conducive work environment, and effective work stress management all contribute to creating an environment that enables individuals to adapt and thrive during times of change.

Recognizing strengths and areas for improvement allows organizations and teams to implement targeted strategies and initiatives that optimize the environment for successful change and enhance overall Changeability.

Putting Adaptability to Work

However, it's important to note that information alone doesn't lead to transformation. I use the data obtained from the AQ® assessment to guide leaders and their teams in doing quick thinking, behavioral, and process changes crucial for achieving rapid results. Together, we leverage the insights gained to build adaptability and enhance change readiness.

With data spanning fifteen dimensions, it's understandable that it can feel overwhelming. You may wonder where to focus, and which areas will have the most significant impact on your priorities. This is where the expertise of an outside consultant/coach comes into play. I have studied the correlations between the measurements and understand which dimensions, when improved, will yield the most positive impact on your specific goals and objectives.

By working together, we can identify the critical areas of focus that will drive the desired outcomes. We will leverage the insights from the assessment to prioritize and address the dimensions that will impact your team's adaptability and change readiness.

The leaders and teams I work with have seen measurable results in retention, innovation, and learning, all contributing to successful operational and technological changes and quantifiable growth and customer impact. We identified individuals who were skilled and motivated to excel during the transition. I also uncovered individuals silently struggling with high levels of work stress, poor emotional well-being, and a diminished sense of support from their team. Not only did this take a toll on their productivity, but it also increased the risk of losing valuable team members.

One of the benefits of this process is that we can identify the individuals within your team who possess a creative mindset and a willingness to learn, innovate, and improve. These individuals are the driving force behind pushing boundaries and exploring new possibilities. On the other hand, we can also identify the steadfast team members who ensure that all changes align with regulations and your established success processes. These individuals provide stability and keep the team grounded.

Understanding your team's level of change readiness allows you to create a workforce better equipped to navigate the challenges of change.

We can also determine your overall team's change readiness and if the organization's environment fosters a culture that promotes change readiness. Focusing on performance, we can also identify where pockets of low resilience, reduced emotional health, and reactivity may lead to conflict or poor team support.

Research shows that promoting employee adaptability is crucial for organizations to stay competitive in our rapidly changing world. Developing a resilient and adaptable workforce can improve revenue growth, shareholder return, and overall success.

By understanding the meaning of adaptability, recognizing its importance in today's world, assessing you and your team's Changeability, and implementing actionable steps, you will be well-equipped to accelerate your and your team's adaptability.

In addition, other actions you can take include:

1. Embrace a Growth Mindset: A growth mindset is the cornerstone of adaptability. Explore practical strategies to foster a growth mindset within yourself and your team. Discover how to shift from a fixed perspective that resists change to one that embraces challenges, values learning, and views setbacks as opportunities for growth.

2. Cultivate Continuous Learning: Adaptability thrives in an environment of continuous learning. Learn how to create a learning culture within your team where curiosity is encouraged, and knowledge is shared. Discover effective methods to promote ongoing skill development and foster a hunger for new information and perspectives.

3. Encourage Flexibility and Experimentation: Adaptability requires flexibility and a willingness to explore new approaches. Explore techniques to encourage flexibility within your team, such as promoting open communication, encouraging idea-sharing, and embracing diverse perspectives. Discover the power of experimentation and how it can fuel innovation and adaptation.

4. Foster Resilience and Agility: Resilience and agility are essential attributes for adaptability. Learn how to build resilience within yourself and your team, enabling you to bounce back from setbacks and adapt quickly to change. Discover strategies for developing agile decision-making and problem-solving skills, helping your team confidently navigate uncertainties.

5. Lead by Example: As a leader, your actions and behaviors set the tone for adaptability within your team. Explore how you can lead by example, demonstrating

adaptability in your approach to work and change. Discover ways to inspire and empower your team members to embrace adaptability, creating a positive and supportive environment for growth.

The Benefits of Developing Adaptability

Developing adaptability brings forth many benefits, empowering individuals to navigate the complexities of a changing world with confidence and resilience. Here are some key advantages that come from cultivating adaptability:

- Enhancing Resilience and Coping Skills: Adaptable individuals possess a heightened ability to bounce back from setbacks and navigate through challenges. By developing resilience, they can effectively cope with unexpected circumstances and recover quickly, maintaining their focus and motivation even in adversity.
- Embracing New Opportunities and Change: Adaptability enables individuals to embrace new opportunities that arise from changes in their personal and professional lives. Rather than being intimidated by unfamiliar situations, adaptable individuals approach them with a sense of curiosity and optimism. They welcome change as a gateway to growth and progress, eagerly seeking ways to learn, evolve, and excel.
- Increasing Personal and Professional Growth: Adaptability catalyzes personal and professional growth. By continuously adapting and learning, individuals can expand their knowledge base, acquire new skills, and develop a broader perspective. They remain open

to new experiences, challenges, and ideas, leading to continuous self-improvement and a more comprehensive range of opportunities.

• Building Confidence and Reducing Fear of the Unknown: Through adaptability, individuals cultivate a sense of self-assurance and confidence in their ability to handle the unknown. By embracing change and developing the flexibility to navigate uncertain circumstances, they become less fearful of the unknown and more willing to take calculated risks. This newfound confidence enables them to seize opportunities and step outside their comfort zones.

It's one thing to read research on paper, it's another to stand witness to the transformation adaptability offers. As a founding certified Adaptability Coach, I have assessed and debriefed over sixty teams and numerous leaders over the past two years. All arrived with a problem to solve, an opportunity to take advantage of, or a result they wished to amplify.

Within the assessment data collected, I partner with leaders to indicate what to leverage in change leadership, which dimensions to leverage to increase exploration, innovation, and the ability to adapt to change, and with this combination, we can add speed and agility to decision making, implementation and adoption of change.

Overall, developing adaptability empowers individuals to thrive in an ever-changing world. By enhancing resilience, embracing change, fostering personal and professional growth, and building confidence, they position themselves for success in their personal and professional lives. Embracing adaptability is not just about surviving in the face of change; it is about thriving, becoming the best version of oneself, and securing your future. An adaptable organization will continue to evolve and stay relevant. It will easily adopt new technology, adjust to market demands and leap ahead of the competition.

Why building an adaptable team is necessary for success

- Rapid Change: Fifty percent of employees will need to be reskilled by 2025 due to changes in technology, market demands and new ways of working (World Economic Forum).
- Talent Adaptability: Employees with a high adaptability are 2.5 times more likely to have higher performance and contribute to the organization's success (McKinsey).
- Innovation: Seventy-nine percent of CEO's consider adaptability and innovation among the top skills they seek in employees to drive business growth (PWC).
- Productivity: Companies with an agile workforce experience a twenty-five percent increase in productivity compared to organizations with less adaptable employees (Korn Ferry).

AQ® or Adaptability Quotient is a measure of individual, team and workplace adaptability. How might your organization measure up?

In this chapter, you learned the importance of adaptability and its relationship with Changeability. AQ® provides clarity on who, how, when and why people adapt.

AQai® defines AQ® as "Measuring the abilities, characteristics and environmental factors which impact the successful behaviors and actions of people, and organizations to effectively respond to uncertainty, new information or changing circumstances." (Decoding AQ®).

If you could improve your adaptability or even the adaptive culture of your organization what might that look like? Take a moment to write down a few observations or take-aways you have learned.

Forward Actions:

1. Curious about your Adaptability? Contact us to take the AQ® assessment, either for yourself or your team. This assessment can provide valuable insights into your current adaptability level and areas that may need improvement. It serves as a baseline for understanding your strengths and weaknesses in adaptability.

2. Continuous Learning and Skill Development: Invest in ongoing learning and skill development. Attend workshops, seminars, or online courses focused on adaptability, change management, and resilience. Encourage your team to do the same. Develop a culture of continuous improvement.

3. Seek Diverse Perspectives: Actively seek out diverse perspectives and opinions when making decisions. Engage with individuals who have different backgrounds, experiences, and viewpoints. This practice can help you adapt to new ideas and approaches more effectively.

4. Practice Scenario Planning: Embrace scenario planning as a strategic tool. Consider various hypothetical scenarios and how your organization would respond to them. This proactive approach can prepare you and your team for unexpected changes and challenges.

5. Encourage Innovation and Experimentation: Foster a culture of innovation and experimentation within your organization. Encourage your team to propose new ideas and solutions without fear of failure. Experimenting with different approaches can enhance adaptability by finding what works best in dynamic situations.

By taking these forward actions, you will not only improve your own adaptability but also create a culture of adaptability within your teams and organizations, ultimately enhancing their ability to thrive in a rapidly changing world.

Turn to the next chapter to learn the art of navigating change with speed and scale. Adaptability concentrates on the capacity to embrace and respond to change. Agility extends this notion, emphasizing the need to do so swiftly and efficiently within a dynamic. Get your seatbelt on, it's time to accelerate forward.

CHAPTER 5

Agility: Unlocking Organizational Agility

*"Change almost never fails because it's too early.
It almost always fails because it's too late."*
—Seth Godin

Raj is a Senior Vice President of a Fortune 500 leading technology firm. His organization values and encourages a growth mindset. From his vantage point, Raj is responsible for leading a successful division within the enterprise and, as long as I have known him, has always had an eye toward the future.

Raj is not afraid to take risks to pursue his vision, even when influencing others may be challenging. Although the company's success is laps ahead of its closest competition, he understands the viability of the company and securing its future depends on its ability to stay relevant and anticipate its customer's changing and future needs.

Read Raj's story and listen for the critical aspects of Changeability: change leadership, adaptability, and agility. Where can you spot them?

"In the shutdown, I had to manage a transition to a new role. As a company, we decided to refocus on what we are good at and focus on our installed base instead of expanding. I found it challenging to lead a new team, especially one with no way to get together physically. I focused on the fact that there were no hallways or cubie conversations. I need to build a connection with my team. I scheduled 1:1's, one hour per day with the team, to share ideas and get to know one another without rush or time pressure. We tried to ramp up communication with the team. I knew communication would be critical for us to keep the team motivated and engaged and our business on target."

A struggle for me was the shift in focus. Although the company was focused on the steady-state business, I saw opportunities to build a business different from the one we were maintaining. The culture needed to 'build the business' differs from the culture needed to 'maintain the business.'

Steady State Culture focuses on execution and efficiencies

and develops deep functional expertise. You are valued for your ability to execute. Building culture is all about experimentation.

You need to run a series of experiments and understand how to target, needing the funding to scale. It is hard for the team to get airtime for that and buy-in. Execution is about organization alignment; the culture helps to convey strategy and execution. In that culture, most focus on skill. You also have to have the right attitude and behaviors. I want people who are excited by the journey, by the vision. To be motivated, not people who stayed in the same silos for twenty years. I want people who have an appetite for new ideas, are ready to learn, and are willing to test the market, not focus on evidence that supports one idea.

We build a strategy with the team, including success factors and operations. We focus on the cultural competencies I need for the people I want to hire.

Raj went on to say "A formal organization is significantly flat and mature. We need functions to support the vision and marketing to craft the right message. We need to be one team, to move quickly and react to what we see in the marketplace.

He continued. "I see an opportunity in the changing marketplace to take advantage of before one of our competitors does. How can we get people on board to adapt and shift the culture's focus to growth versus maintenance? I need to be one level higher in the organization, reporting to the CEO for influence. I need senior leadership directly engaged in selling to a new customer. I need buy-in, alignment, and conviction from the CEO; however, taking the time to develop it slows the team down."

Big decisions need to be made. Raj decided he needed to:

o   Build market knowledge.
o   Gain intimate knowledge of the strategy.
o   Opt-in and opt out of what fits the strategy quickly.

He continued to say "I look to hire the right people who are turned on by the vision and have the grit to achieve it. Then, I look at their accomplishments. That is the most significant hallmark."

As a change leader, Raj knows the value of aligning the team to the vision. He realizes he must influence critical stakeholders to have his ideas acted upon. He navigates the politics, policies, and protocols as needed while delivering the business outcomes required from his division. Leveraging his skill of Changeability, he understands the importance of having a change-ready team who can adapt as needed, recognizing that his customers' current and future needs will change. Therefore, he only hires team members ready for change, willing to unlearn and let go of old successes to risk moving forward. He sees adaptability and agility as critical pillars to sustain the company's growth. Although successful, he refuses to lose an inch of ground to the competitors in his rear-view mirror.

Raj embodies the values of a growth mindset and forward-thinking. Raj is one of my favorite clients. He understands that staying relevant and securing the future of his company depends on its ability to anticipate and meet the changing needs of its customers. Raj's story serves as an insightful example of the critical aspects of Changeability: change leadership, adaptability, and agility. Let's dive into his experiences and draw valuable lessons on the path to agility.

- Navigating Change in a Remote Environment: During a company shutdown, Raj faced the challenge of transitioning to a new role while leading a team that could no longer interact physically. Recognizing the absence of informal conversations, he prioritized building connections. Raj scheduled one-on-one meetings, allowing time for idea-sharing and team building. Open communication became key to maintaining collaboration and cohesion in a remote setting.

- Balancing Steady-State Focus and Growth Opportunities: As the company shifted its focus to the steady-state business, Raj saw untapped potential for building a different business model. He acknowledged the difference in cultures required for maintaining versus building a business. While steady-state culture emphasizes execution and efficiency, building culture centers around experimentation. Raj sought individuals motivated by the journey, with an appetite for new ideas and a willingness to test the market.

- Fostering a Culture of Growth: To rally his team around a growth-focused culture, Raj aligned the strategy with cultural competencies. He emphasized the importance of hiring individuals who shared the vision and demonstrated the grit to achieve it. Market knowledge, strategy immersion, and quick decision-making became paramount as Raj aimed to shift the culture and seize opportunities in a changing marketplace.

- Influencing Stakeholders and Gaining Alignment: As a change leader, Raj understood the significance of influencing critical stakeholders to support his ideas. Navigating through politics, policies, and protocols, he ensured the team's efforts aligned with the overall vision. Raj recognized the need for buy-in, alignment, and conviction from the CEO. However, he balanced the urgency of making big decisions with the importance of developing market knowledge and strategy alignment.

- Embracing Adaptability and Agility: Raj firmly believed in the importance of adaptability and agility as pillars for sustained growth. He sought team members who were ready to embrace change, unlearn outdated practices, and take risks. Raj's focus on adaptability and agility allowed his team to respond quickly to evolving customer needs and maintain a competitive edge in the marketplace.

Raj's journey exemplifies the power of change leadership, adaptability, and agility in driving sustained growth. By navigating change in a remote environment, balancing steady-state focus and growth opportunities, fostering a culture of growth, influencing stakeholders, and embracing adaptability and agility, Raj successfully positioned his team for success. His story serves as an inspiration for leaders seeking to build agile teams and organizations that can navigate change and seize opportunities.

Redefining Agility for Success in a Dynamic Business Landscape

In this chapter explore the concept of agility as a foundational driver for your team or organization's success. Agility, the third essential component of Changeability, plays a pivotal role in empowering you and your team or organization to not only thrive but excel. It transcends mere reactions to change; it encompasses the aptitude to act swiftly, adapt readily, and respond effectively within a dynamic environment.

Our approach extends beyond the confines of agile methodologies and frameworks, placing a spotlight on your team's capacity to navigate a continuously evolving environment with speed and effectiveness. This capacity draws upon the skills and capabilities that we've been developing throughout the previous chapters dedicated to Changeability, change leadership, and adaptability.

What is Agility?

Agility within Changeability refers to the ability to move quickly, adapt readily, and respond effectively in a changing and uncertain environment. It goes beyond merely reacting to change and involves a proactive and dynamic approach that allows individuals, teams, and organizations to thrive amidst complexity and uncertainty. Embracing uncertainty means creating an environment where individuals feel comfortable facing the unknown and are empowered to adapt quickly.

Agility is characterized by a mindset that embraces new ideas, experimentation, and ambiguity. It necessitates assessing situations, making informed decisions, and taking real-time actions. Agile individuals and teams adjust their plans and strategies based on evolving circumstances, remaining adaptable, innovative, and resilient.

Within the context of Changeability, agility encompasses developing an agile mindset, cultivating skills and capabilities, and embracing uncertainty. It is essential for seizing opportunities, responding to customer needs, and staying ahead of competitors. As a change leader, you play a pivotal role in fostering an agile mindset by promoting growth, openness to new ideas, and a willingness to experiment. Organizations that focus on building the necessary skills, such as effective communication, collaboration, problem-solving, critical thinking, and decision-making, are better positioned to become more agile.

By creating an environment where individuals feel comfortable embracing uncertainty and are empowered to adapt quickly, you cultivate a culture of flexibility, experimentation, and resilience. This agility is a cornerstone for your team or organization's continued success in today's dynamic business landscape.

You can build the skills of change leadership and promote a culture of adaptability but without the ability to move quickly, agility, you, your team or your organization might fall behind. Deadlines are missed, customers are impacted and the competition speeds on by.

Overcoming Barriers to Team Agility

Several factors can hinder team agility. These barriers can prevent teams from fully embracing agility and impede their ability to respond quickly and effectively to change. Below are common obstacles that impede team agility.

Resistance to change: A significant barrier to team agility is resistance. When team members are resistant or hesitant to embrace new ideas, processes, or working methods, it can slow down the team's ability to adapt and respond. Overcoming resistance to change requires effective change management. Overcome resistance by explaining why the change is needed, how it will apply to them and what is needed for their support. Be transparent, share your worries about the change and ask how together you and your team will overcome them.

1. Siloed mentality: When teams operate in silos, with limited collaboration and communication across departments or functions, it hampers agility. Silos create barriers to information sharing, coordination, and collective decision-making. To foster agility, teams must break down silos, promote cross-functional

collaboration, and create a culture of shared ownership and goals.

2. Inflexible processes and structures: Rigid processes and hierarchical structures can hinder agility. When teams are bound by strict workflows, approval processes, or reporting structures, it becomes challenging to respond quickly to change. There is a lessened opportunity to grow risk intelligence. Agile teams require flexibility in their processes and the autonomy to make decisions and take action within their domain.

3. Lack of empowerment and autonomy: Team members who lack empowerment and autonomy may struggle to exhibit agility. When individuals feel micromanaged or unable to make decisions, it stifles their ability to act swiftly and adapt. Encouraging a culture of trust, empowerment, and decentralized decision-making can remove this barrier and enable team agility.

4. Limited access to resources and support: Insufficient resources, whether budget, time, or technology, can impede agility. Teams need the tools, resources, and support to navigate change effectively. Providing adequate resources and ensuring teams have access to the support they need are crucial for fostering agility.

5. Resistance to learning and continuous improvement: Agility is closely tied to a learning mindset and constant improvement. It can only hinder agility if team members refrain from learning new skills, exploring innovative approaches, or reflecting on their performance. Cultivating a culture of continuous learning, encouraging experimentation, and recognizing the value of ongoing improvement is essential for team agility.

Addressing these barriers requires a holistic approach, including leadership support, organizational culture change, and targeted interventions. By removing these obstacles, your team and organization can enhance their agility and unleash their full potential to navigate change, seize opportunities, and drive success.

Turning Obstacles into Opportunities

So what can you do to increase your team's agility?

1. Empower Individuals: Agile environments empower individuals to take ownership of their work and make decisions. By providing autonomy and trust, teams can tap into their full potential and bring their unique strengths. Empowered individuals are more likely to embrace change, take initiative, and contribute to the team's agility.

2. Continuous Learning and Skill Development: Agility requires a mindset of constant learning and skill development. Organizations and teams that prioritize learning and provide growth opportunities foster a culture of agility. Encouraging individuals to expand their knowledge, acquire new skills, and stay abreast of industry trends equips them to adapt and thrive in a rapidly changing landscape. Prioritize learning and growth opportunities to foster a culture of agility.

3. Emotional Intelligence and Collaboration: Developing mental fitness and Emotional intelligence (EQ) fosters collaboration and effective teamwork. Agile individuals possess strong EQ, enabling them to understand and navigate emotions, build relationships, and communicate

effectively. Emotionally intelligent individuals are more likely to embrace diverse perspectives, resolve conflicts, and foster a positive team culture.

4. Change Leadership: Agility requires strong change leadership from individuals at all levels. Change leaders inspire and motivate others, guide the team through transitions, and create an environment conducive to change. They facilitate the adoption of new ideas, champion continuous improvement, and ensure alignment with the organization's strategic objectives. Share the head, heart and hands model of change leadership with your team.

5. Resilience and Adaptability: Agile individuals exhibit adaptability when facing challenges and setbacks. They embrace change as an opportunity for growth, quickly recover from failures, and proactively seek solutions. Resilient individuals are more likely to bounce back from adversity and continue driving towards team goals, enhancing overall agility.

6. Building Trust and Psychological Safety: Trust and psychological safety are essential components of an agile team. When individuals feel safe expressing their opinions, taking risks, and making mistakes without fear of judgment or negative consequences, they are more willing to contribute and collaborate effectively. Building trust and psychological safety fosters a culture of openness, innovation, and agility.

Building the foundation of Changeability lays a strong foundation for agility. By focusing on the people side of agility and nurturing the above qualities, teams can unlock their full potential and maximize their agility. Organizations that prioritize the development and well-being of their team members create an environment that supports adaptability, innovation, and sustained success.

Breaking Down Silos for Enhanced Agility

A threat I continue to see is siloed organizations. Silos, both physical and metaphorical, can hinder agility within organizations. Silos refer to isolated departments, teams, or individuals that operate independently, limiting collaboration, communication, and the flow of information. Breaking down silos is crucial for fostering agility, as it encourages cross-functional collaboration, knowledge sharing, and a collective sense of purpose.

Sometimes trying to get teams to collaborate is too much to bear. This led a Director of Engineering to give up the role of people leader and business collaborator. Stakeholder relationships are complex enough without the siloed thinking and priorities of departments needing to collaborate.

Here's why breaking down silos is vital for enhancing agility:

1. Enhanced Communication and Collaboration: Silos often lead to communication gaps and limited collaboration between different parts of the organization. By breaking down these silos, teams can communicate more effectively, share knowledge, and work collaboratively towards common goals. This cross-functional collaboration facilitates agility by enabling faster decision-making, problem-solving, and innovation.

2. Improved Information Flow: Silos create barriers to the flow of information, impeding agility. When

departments or teams work in isolation, essential insights and updates may get lost or delayed, hindering the organization's ability to respond swiftly to market changes. Breaking down silos ensures a seamless flow of information across teams, enabling faster and more informed decision-making.

3. Holistic View of the Customer: Silos can prevent organizations from comprehensively understanding their customers. When information is siloed, different departments may have limited visibility into customer needs, preferences, and pain points. Breaking down silos allows for a holistic view of the customer, enabling organizations to tailor their products, services, and strategies to meet evolving customer demands and preferences.

4. Flexibility and Adaptability: Silos often result in rigid structures and processes, making it difficult to adapt quickly to changing market conditions. By breaking down silos, organizations foster flexibility and adaptability. Teams can collaborate across functions, share resources, and realign their efforts to respond rapidly to market shifts, emerging trends, and customer demands.

5. Encouraging a Culture of Learning and Innovation: Silos can stifle organizational innovation and learning. When teams operate in isolation, knowledge and ideas may remain confined within their respective silos, limiting the cross-pollination of ideas and hindering innovation. Breaking down silos encourages a culture of learning and innovation, where diverse perspectives and ideas are shared, leading to creative problem-solving and continuous improvement.

To break down silos and enhance agility, organizations can implement several strategies:

- Foster a Shared Vision and Common Goals: Establish shared visions and goals that transcend departmental boundaries, aligning everyone towards a common purpose.

- Encourage Cross-Functional Teams: Form cross-functional teams to tackle complex projects or challenges, bringing together individuals from different departments to collaborate and share expertise.

- Promote Open Communication Channels: Implement communication channels that facilitate information sharing and collaboration across departments, such as digital platforms, regular meetings, and knowledge-sharing sessions.

- Provide Learning and Development Opportunities: Offer training and development programs encouraging individuals to broaden their skills and knowledge, fostering a cross-functional understanding and collaboration culture.

- Recognize and Reward Collaboration: Recognize and reward behaviors that promote collaboration, teamwork, and knowledge sharing to reinforce a culture that values cross-functional cooperation.

With increased collaboration, organizations can unlock the full potential of their teams, enhancing agility and enabling them to respond quickly and effectively to change. Breaking down silos is an ongoing process that requires continuous effort and commitment, but the rewards in terms of enhanced agility and improved organizational performance are well worth the investment.

Cultivating Skills and Capabilities for Agility

In the pursuit of agility, mindset alone is not enough; cultivating the right skills and capabilities is equally crucial. Building a skill set for agility empowers individuals and teams to effectively navigate change and capitalize on emerging opportunities. Some of the critical skills and abilities that contribute to agility include:

Collaboration and Communication: Agile teams thrive on effective collaboration and communication. Skills like active listening, empathy, and providing constructive feedback are essential for fostering cohesion within teams and driving innovation. Active listening goes beyond hearing words; it involves understanding the emotions and perspectives behind the words, facilitating deeper connections and more meaningful problem-solving discussions. Empathetic communication encourages team members to relate to each other's experiences and challenges, creating a supportive environment for idea generation. Constructive feedback, on the other hand, promotes continuous improvement, refining ideas and approaches, ultimately enhancing a team's agility.

Problem-solving and Critical Thinking: Agility necessitates critical thinking and the ability to solve complex problems. Developing skills in situation analysis, root cause identification, and creative solution generation enhances the agility of decision-making. Encouraging employees to contribute solutions through facilitated action-focused groups fosters a psychologically safe environment for insight gathering. This approach yields quicker results in problem-solving, empowering clients to address challenges efficiently.

Flexibility and Adaptability: Cultivating adaptability and flexibility skills equips individuals and teams to respond swiftly to changing circumstances and make necessary course corrections. By understanding the dimensions of adaptability, leaders and teams can readily apply them to navigate change effectively.

Resilience and Stress Management: Resilience and stress management capabilities are essential for agile individuals and teams. These skills enable them to bounce back from setbacks and effectively handle stress. Prioritizing self-care, stress management, and nurturing a positive mindset enhances overall well-being and equips individuals to cope with stress more effectively, maintaining composure and clear thinking during high-pressure situations.

The Role of Decision-Making: Consider the speed of decision-making in your organization. While artificial intelligence and data provide faster decision-making guidance, many organizations experience delays in decision-making processes. Why is this the case? Often, organizations operate in complex, matrixed structures where decisions involve multiple departments and stakeholders.

In agile environments, the speed of decision-making is critical. Agile teams navigate fast-paced, dynamic landscapes where delays in decision-making can impede progress and responsiveness. Effective decision-making is integral to agility, enabling teams to adapt promptly, respond effectively, and seize opportunities. It ensures alignment with goals, allows necessary course corrections, and facilitates successful change navigation.

Techniques for Quick and Effective Decision-Making: To enhance rapid decision-making, employ strategies that facilitate efficient and effective choices. Consider implementing these methods:

Clear Roles and Decision Authorities: Define decision-making roles and authorities within the team, establishing a framework for swift decision-making. Clarity ensures that decisions are made by the appropriate individuals, reducing delays and confusion.

Decentralized Decision-Making: Empower team members to make decisions within their areas of expertise, promoting agility. Decentralizing decision-making allows teams to respond quickly to emerging situations without relying on hierarchical approval processes, fostering autonomy and accountability.

Decision Frameworks: Utilize decision frameworks, such as the RAPID framework (Responsible, Accountable, Consulted, Informed), to streamline decision-making. These frameworks offer a structured approach to identifying decision-makers, gathering stakeholder input, and reaching consensus efficiently.

Agile Rituals: Incorporate agile rituals like daily stand-up meetings and sprint retrospectives to facilitate regular communication and decision-making opportunities. These rituals enable teams to address emerging issues, make quick decisions, and adapt their strategies as needed.

Cultivating Skills and Capabilities for Agility:
While mindset is essential, cultivating the right skills and capabilities is equally crucial for agility. Building a skill set for agility enables individuals and teams to navigate change and

respond to emerging opportunities. Some critical skills and abilities to cultivate for agility include:

1. Collaboration and Communication: Agile teams thrive on collaboration and effective communication. Developing skills in active listening, empathy, and constructive feedback enables teams to work together cohesively and foster innovation. For instance, active listening involves not only hearing words but also understanding the emotions and perspectives behind them. This can lead to deeper connections among team members and more meaningful problem-solving discussions. Additionally, empathetic communication helps team members relate to each other's experiences and challenges, creating a supportive environment where ideas can flow freely. Lastly, providing constructive feedback allows for continuous improvement, as it helps team members refine their ideas and approaches, ultimately enhancing the team's agility and adaptability.

2. Problem-solving and Critical Thinking: Agility requires thinking critically and solving complex problems. Developing skills in analyzing situations, identifying root causes, and generating creative solutions enhances agility in decision-making. Many times I have facilitated small action focused groups whose purpose was to problem solve or to accelerate taking advantage of an opportunity. This creates an environment of psychological safety, providing laser focused solutions through insight gathering. I find giving employees the opportunity to provide the solutions yields a faster result. Teaching them how to build a business case, make informed critical decisions and to listen and share

diverse ideas bulbs the platform for critical thinking and problem solving. As a result my clients gain solutions to problems faster than they thought possible.

3. Flexibility and Adaptability: Building skills in adaptability and flexibility allows individuals and teams to adjust quickly to changing circumstances and make necessary course corrections. Leaders and teams can quickly understand the dimensions of adaptability and apply them.

4. Resilience and Stress Management: Agile individuals and teams need resilience to rebound from setbacks and adeptly handle stress. Developing capabilities in self-care, stress management, and nurturing a positive mindset bolsters agility when confronted with challenges. For instance, focusing on self-care not only promotes overall well-being but also equips individuals to cope with stress more effectively. Talk about stress as an avatar. How does it enter the department, what feeds it? What releases it, how can its pressure be reduced? Stress management techniques enable individuals to maintain composure and clear thinking during high-pressure situations.

Gain Speed and Scale by Embracing Uncertainty and Adapting Quickly to Change

Uncertainty is a constant in today's business environment, and agility requires embracing it with a proactive and adaptive approach. Embracing uncertainty involves:

1. Anticipating Change: Agile individuals and teams stay ahead by anticipating and preparing for potential

changes. This involves monitoring industry trends, conducting continuous market research, and proactively seeking insights and information.

2. Rapid Decision-Making: Agility calls for making quick and informed decisions. Embracing uncertainty means having the ability to gather and analyze relevant information swiftly and make timely decisions to respond to changing circumstances.

3. Iterative Approach: Agility encourages an iterative approach to change. Rather than seeking perfection from the start, agile individuals and teams embrace experimentation, learning from failures and making iterative improvements to achieve desired outcomes.

By developing an agile mindset, cultivating skills and capabilities for agility, and embracing uncertainty, individuals and teams can enhance their ability to adapt quickly and thrive in a rapidly evolving business environment.

Leveraging Data and Insights to Inform Decisions:

Data and insights are valuable resources for informed decision-making in agile environments. Leveraging data helps teams make data-driven decisions that reduce bias and increase accuracy. Some strategies to leverage data and insights effectively include:

1. Data Analytics: Utilizing data analytics tools and techniques enables teams to gain meaningful insights from large datasets. Analyzing patterns, trends, and customer behavior provides a foundation for informed decision-making.

2. Customer Feedback and User Testing: Incorporating customer feedback and user testing into the decision-making process helps teams validate ideas and identify opportunities for improvement. By gathering feedback early and iteratively, teams can quickly adjust and align their decisions with customer needs.

3. Experimentation and Learning Loops: Adopting an experimental mindset and implementing learning loops allows teams to test hypotheses, gather feedback, and iterate rapidly. This approach facilitates evidence-based decision-making and encourages a culture of continuous improvement.

By employing these techniques and leveraging data and insights, teams can make rapid and effective decisions that align with their goals and drive agility. Fast decision-making is a critical component of agility, enabling teams to seize opportunities, adapt to change, and stay ahead of the competition. The upcoming sections of this chapter will explore practical strategies and tools to enhance your rapid decision-making skills and promote agility within your team and organization.

Building Collaborative and Cross-Functional Teams:

Agile environments thrive on collaboration and cross-functional teamwork. Building collaborative teams involves bringing together individuals with diverse skills, backgrounds, and perspectives to foster creativity, innovation, and collective problem-solving. Some strategies for building collaborative and cross-functional teams include:

1. Clear Roles and Responsibilities: Clearly defining roles and responsibilities within the team establishes clarity and accountability. Each team member should understand their contributions and how their skills complement others, promoting effective collaboration.

2. Encouraging Psychological Safety: Creating a psychologically safe environment fosters collaboration. Team members should feel comfortable sharing their ideas, taking risks, and challenging assumptions without fear of judgment or retribution. Psychological safety encourages open dialogue and idea-sharing, leading to more effective collaboration.

3. Cross-Functional Pairing and Rotation: Encouraging cross-functional pairing and rotation allows team members to learn from one another, broaden their skill sets, and gain a deeper understanding of different perspectives. This practice promotes knowledge sharing, collaboration, and a shared sense of ownership.

These strategies can significantly enhance collaboration within teams, ultimately contributing to agility and the ability to adapt quickly to changing circumstances.

Effective Communication in Agile Environments:

Effective communication is fundamental in agile environments, where collaboration and adaptability are essential. Clear and timely communication ensures that information flows seamlessly within the team, promoting alignment and facilitating quick decision-making. Consider the following practices for effective communication:

1. Transparent and Open Communication: Encourage open and transparent communication channels within the team. Foster a culture where team members feel comfortable sharing their thoughts, concerns, and progress updates. Transparent communication promotes trust and facilitates collaboration.

2. Regular Stand-Up Meetings: Daily stand-up meetings allow team members to synchronize their activities, identify any roadblocks, and foster a shared understanding of progress and priorities. These short, focused meetings encourage collaboration and alignment.

3. Visual Communication and Information Radiators: Visual aids such as Kanban boards, burndown charts, or task boards can enhance communication and create a shared understanding of progress and work items. Information radiators provide transparency and visibility into the team's progress and help identify potential bottlenecks or areas for improvement.

Harnessing the Power of Collective Intelligence:

Agile environments leverage the collective intelligence of the team, recognizing that individuals' combined knowledge and expertise can lead to better outcomes. Harnessing the power of collective intelligence involves:

1. Encouraging Knowledge Sharing: Create opportunities for knowledge sharing within the team, such as lunch-and-learn sessions, workshops, or communities of practice. Encouraging team members to share their expertise and learn from one another enhances collaboration and drives innovation.

2. Facilitating Retrospectives: Regular retrospectives enable the team to reflect on their processes, successes, and areas for improvement. Retrospectives promote continuous learning and collective problem-solving by providing a safe space for open and honest feedback.

3. Embracing Diverse Perspectives: Recognize and value diverse perspectives within the team. Different backgrounds, experiences, and expertise contribute to a more holistic and comprehensive approach to problem-solving. Embracing diverse perspectives fosters innovation and drives better outcomes.

By building collaborative and cross-functional teams, establishing effective communication practices, and harnessing the power of collective intelligence, teams can enhance their agility. Collaboration and communication form the bedrock of agile environments, enabling teams to adapt, innovate, and thrive in the face of change. In the upcoming sections, we will explore practical strategies and techniques to strengthen collaboration and communication within your team, fostering agility and driving success.

Embracing Changeability: The Key to Achieving Agile Transformation

Many of my clients have the goal of building an agile culture. They also wish to maximize risk intelligence. We want people to move faster and to experiment, yet do so within the guardrails of compliance. To fully grow Changeability in any environment, from an innovative start-up to a decades old established organization, in addition to the above, I rank several options as the core of Changeability.

1. Change Champions and Influencers: Agility within an organization can be amplified by identifying and empowering change champions and influencers. These individuals play a crucial role in driving change, inspiring others, and modeling the behaviors needed for agility. By recognizing and supporting these change agents, organizations can create a network of advocates to foster a culture of change and agility.

2. Continuous Feedback and Learning Loops: Incorporating ongoing feedback mechanisms and learning loops into the organizational culture promotes agility. Encouraging individuals to provide feedback, reflect on their experiences, and apply lessons learned enables continuous improvement and adaptation. Learning loops can be established through retrospectives, post-implementation reviews, and regular feedback sessions.

3. Agility as a Leadership Competency: Leadership plays a vital role in shaping the people's side of agility. Leaders who demonstrate agility as a competency inspire and guide their teams toward embracing change, adapting quickly, and driving innovation. Developing leadership capabilities that align with agility, such as visionary thinking, flexibility, and empowering others, reinforces the people side of agility.

4. Diversity and Inclusion: Embracing diversity and inclusion is essential for fostering agility. A diverse workforce brings a variety of perspectives, experiences, and ideas, fueling creativity and innovation. Inclusive environments that value and leverage diverse voices encourage collaboration and enable organizations to navigate change with agility.

5. Continuous Employee Engagement: Actively engaging employees throughout the change journey promotes their buy-in and commitment to agility. Regular communication, involvement in decision-making, and providing opportunities for growth and development contribute to a sense of ownership and engagement. Engaged employees are likely to embrace change, contribute ideas, and drive agility within their teams.

6. Agile Talent Management: Agility requires a talent management approach that aligns with the principles of flexibility and adaptability. This includes flexible work arrangements, cross-training and upskilling opportunities, and promoting internal mobility. Agile talent management ensures the organization has the right skills and capabilities to respond to changing needs and challenges.

By integrating these aspects into your Changeability framework, you can strengthen the people's side of agility and create an environment where individuals are empowered, engaged, and capable of driving and embracing change. Remember, agility is not solely about processes and tools; it is ultimately about the people who embody and enable agility within the organization.

The Impact of Agility

Organizations are constantly seeking ways to enhance their competitiveness and adaptability. One powerful approach that has gained significant traction is the adoption of agile methodologies. These methodologies offer a dynamic framework for organizations to respond swiftly to changes, innovate, and deliver exceptional results. The following statistics shed light on the remarkable benefits that organizations can realize through the implementation of agile practices. By increasing productivity, improving project success rates, boosting customer satisfaction, fostering innovation, and reducing time-to-market, agile methodologies empower organizations to thrive in an increasingly competitive and unpredictable business environment.

Organizations that successfully use an agile framework/system gain several benefits.

Organizations that have successfully implemented agile methodologies see a 40% increase in productivity and a 46% increase in project success rates compared to traditional methods and report a 33% increase in customer satisfaction compared to non-agile organizations. Companies that adopt agile practices are more innovative, with 62% of agile organizations reporting significant or very high levels of innovation compared to only 28% of non-agile organizations. They reduce time to market by up to 50% allowing them to release new products and services faster and stay ahead of the competition. In addition, according to a survey of 1,500 organizations, 74% of respondents reported that agile practices had improved their team's ability to manage changing priorities. These statistics demonstrate the benefits that organizations can enjoy by adopting agile methodologies. By increasing productivity, project success rates, and customer satisfaction while promoting innovation and reducing time-to-market, agile methods can help organizations stay competitive and adapt to changing market conditions.

Your Role in Leading an Agile Team

As a leader, you play a crucial role in fostering agility within your team. In today's rapidly changing business landscape, navigating uncertainty, adapting quickly, and seizing opportunities are essential for success. By embracing your role as an agile leader, you have the power to inspire and empower your team to thrive in dynamic environments, achieve remarkable outcomes, and stay ahead of the competition.

Create a culture of openness and experimentation: Encourage agility by creating a culture that values experimentation and learning. This can involve giving team members the freedom to try new things, rewarding risk-taking, and fostering an environment where failure is seen as an opportunity for growth. Agile leaders focus on serving their teams and removing obstacles that could slow progress. In addition, they prioritize empowering their teams to work autonomously and collaboratively.

One of my clients' organizations schedules a "Future's Meeting," which discusses the impact of change and possible changes on their organization. I will be facilitating a discussion on the implications of AI in their industry. Ask questions such as "What impact will artificial intelligence (AI) have on the production, research and development, delivery, and ongoing support of the products and services you offer?" One client renamed their conference room and virtual banner for Zoom to "Think Tank" to spur creative ideas.

Provide clear goals and priorities: Leaders can increase agility by providing clear goals and priorities that help team members focus their efforts and make progress. This can involve setting specific, measurable goals and regularly communicating progress. Use my "Debora-ism" by asking, "Who will do what by when, and how will I or we know?"

A high-performing leader in an organization was asked to join an underperforming department and tasked with its turnaround. He immediately saw all that needed to be improved. In our meeting, he expressed his concern about the state of the department and the lengthy list of priorities he shared with me. I gave him a challenge. I asked him to share the list and desired outcomes with the department and clearly state his goals. Much to his surprise, the team readily embraced the tasks, each took on a role and a piece of the project, and my client was left only with the job of motivating, coaching, and supporting the team versus doing the task.

The tasks were completed faster than expected, and the team expressed pride in their accomplishments. My client was recognized for his ability to improve operations, customer impact, and profitability quickly.

Foster teamwork, collaboration, and communication: You can promote agility by fostering a culture of collaboration and communication. This can involve encouraging cross-functional teams, facilitating communication channels, and creating opportunities for team members to share ideas and feedback. Agile leadership emphasizes teamwork and collaboration among team members over individual heroics. Empower your teams to make decisions.

An enterprise-wide division of a payment technology company was incurring slow decision-making. Meetings upon meetings were held, reviewing the same topics repeatedly without an actionable conclusion. After speaking with several stakeholders and team members, I discovered the root of the delay. The leader's team needed to be made aware of the decision filters their leader used when making a decision. Fearing making the wrong decision, they decided not to, leaving the final choice to their superior. I coached the leader to share his decision filters and the process he uses to make decisions. Once he did, decisions accelerated, and he found the team's ideas were on par with the organization's goals.

Invest in training and development: Leaders can increase agility by investing in training and development programs that help team members build skills and stay up-to-date with the latest trends and technologies. This can involve providing access to training resources, mentorship programs, or external training programs. Offer opportunities for experimentation by creating innovation teams. Our action focus groups often solve the biggest organizational problems or implement the most significant improvements within ninety days or less.

Emphasize continuous improvement: Leaders can promote agility by emphasizing the importance of constant improvement. This can involve regular retrospectives or post-project reviews, where teams reflect on their processes and identify areas for improvement. Focus both on improvement and transformation.

Lastly, lead by example. You can increase agility by modeling agile behaviors themselves. This can involve being open to change, embracing experimentation, and fostering a culture of continuous improvement.

Overall, increase agility in your teams by creating a culture of openness, collaboration, and continuous improvement. By fostering these values, you will help your teams adapt quickly to changing circumstances, experiment with new ideas, and deliver high-quality work efficiently.

Forward Action:

1. Practice Rapid Decision-Making: Practice the 3-5-10 brainstorming method. Identify a problem or opportunity you want to solve. Generate three ideas in three minutes by yourself. Pair up with another person and generate five ideas each within five minutes. Write all ideas on a sticky note. In ten minutes, in a large group, place all sticky notes on a whiteboard. Cluster similar ideas. Vote and decide.

2. Cultivate a Learning Mindset: Embrace a continuous learning mindset within yourself and your team. Encourage a culture of learning from both successes and failures to adapt and grow. Develop forward thinking by asking "what would our competitor do faster in this situation?"

3. Implement Agile Processes: Explore agile methodologies and consider implementing them in your work or organization. Agile frameworks can enhance adaptability and efficiency.

4. Enhance Cross-Functional Collaboration: Foster collaboration and communication across different teams and departments. Break down silos to improve agility in your organization's response to change. Exchange a virtual coffee or an informal meeting with your peers.

5. Monitor and Adapt to Trends: Stay vigilant about industry and market trends. Regularly assess the external landscape to proactively adapt strategies and seize emerging opportunities.

Agility harmoniously aligns with the principles explored in our previous chapters dedicated to change leadership and adaptability, collectively forming the broader concept of Changeability.

While change leadership equips you with the skills and strategies to initiate and guide transformative processes, adaptability fosters the capacity to adjust and respond to evolving circumstances. Agility, as the third pillar of Changeability, complements these facets by emphasizing the swiftness, dynamism, and proactive approach necessary to navigate change effectively.

Together, they create a comprehensive framework that empowers individuals, teams, and organizations to not only embrace change but to thrive in an ever-shifting landscape.

CHAPTER 6

Elevating Agility and Adaptability with AI

> *Building advanced AI is like launching a rocket. The first challenge is to maximize acceleration, but once it starts picking up speed, you also need to focus on steering.*
>
> —Jaan Tallinn

A lex had built a strong reputation in the industry for his ability to protect organizations against cyber threats. He had worked his way up the ladder through years of hard work and dedication and had earned the trust of his colleagues and customers alike.

However, over time, Alex began to realize that the world of cyber security was changing rapidly. More and more organizations were turning to artificial intelligence (AI) and machine learning to help detect and prevent cyber-attacks. Alex knew he needed to develop new skills to stay relevant but needed help finding the time and resources.

Alex's lack of AI skills soon became a liability despite his best efforts. Clients began to demand that their cyber security providers be able to integrate AI into their services, and competitors who had embraced this technology were starting to outperform Alex's company. Alex's team tried to compensate by hiring AI experts, but they needed help to keep up with the pace of change.

Eventually, the writing was on the wall. Alex was called into a meeting with the company's senior leaders and told he would be let go. He was not a good model for the rest of his team. They thanked him for his contributions to the company but clarified that his failure to develop AI skills had made him no longer competitive.

Feeling lost and dejected, Alex spent some time reflecting on his career and where he had gone wrong. He realized he had become complacent and needed to adapt to the changing cybersecurity landscape. Alex also recognized that he had not prioritized his professional development, instead relying on his existing knowledge and experience to carry him through. He had failed to build a power base of internal relationships in his busyness, so there wasn't anyone to advocate for him.

With a newfound determination, Alex began to immerse himself in AI and cyber security. He took courses, attended conferences, and reached out to experts in the field. Over time, he became an AI expert in his own right and started his own consulting business focused on helping organizations integrate AI into their cybersecurity strategies.

Although losing his job had been a challenging and humbling experience, Alex was grateful for the wake-up call. He realized that the world of cyber security was constantly evolving and that he needed to remain agile and adaptable to stay relevant. With his new skills and knowledge, he was confident that he could succeed in the industry again; this time, he would not let himself fall behind.

Leveraging AI to Excel

By the time you are reading this, AI may have already become a mainstream phenomenon, integrated into various aspects of your personal and professional life. However, it's essential to acknowledge that the rapid pace of technological advancement means that a new disruption might already be on the frontier. AI, while currently in the spotlight, could merely be the flavor of the day.

As a leader with the skills of change leadership, adaptability, and agility, you can navigate through such transformative periods. You can use these skills to guide your teams through uncertainty, instill confidence, and foster resilience.

AI is only one example of change. With all disruptive technologies, organizations will face the challenge of identifying the risks and benefits. One thing is clear: to stay relevant, you must develop the mindset and skills to adapt to any disruption.

AI and Change Leadership

One of my favorite resources is the online magazine, *Strategy+Business*, which recently explored how individuals can use AI to improve the change management process and what skills change leaders need to develop to leverage AI in *AI and the Future of Change Management* by Greg Verdino.

The skills required for change leaders include understanding the potential of AI, using it to leverage its potential, and evaluating and selecting appropriate AI technologies. This means developing stakeholder relationships and collaborating with data scientists and IT teams to effectively communicate and reap AI benefits.

Regarding Artificial Intelligence (AI), opinions among my clients vary. Some are brimming with excitement about its potential to revolutionize their industries. I recently received enthusiastic emails from a CEO who proudly shared how his company has successfully integrated AI into its operations, boosting efficiency and innovation. On the other hand, only some are equally convinced. One of my clients expressed concerns about his technology team dismissing AI as a fad. He worries that their reluctance to embrace AI might hinder their ability to capitalize on its opportunities, particularly in a highly change-oriented field like disruptive technology.

Reflecting on these contrasting perspectives, it becomes evident that attitudes toward AI can shape an organization's approach to change and innovation. The question remains: how do you feel about artificial intelligence? Are you excited about its potential to drive transformation, or do you doubt its impact on your team and industry? Understanding your stance on AI is crucial as you navigate the ever-evolving landscape of technological advancements and prepare your team for the changes.

How will AI benefit you?

AI can transform the way you work and make decisions by providing new sources of data and insights that enable you to be more informed, efficient, and effective. AI offers the opportunity to analyze large volumes of data and detect patterns and trends that may not be immediately apparent to humans; AI provides a more comprehensive understanding of your environment, enabling you to make better data-driven decisions and act quickly and proactively. AI can also automate routine tasks and processes, freeing up time and resources to focus on higher-level strategic issues.

Imagine facilitating collaboration more quickly and learning and developing new skills more efficiently, helping you and your team stay ahead of the curve and adapt to changing circumstances. Using AI can enable your team to be more agile, innovative, and effective in a rapidly changing environment. You can deliver value to your organization with less effort and greater focus, assuring you will never have a meeting like the one experienced by Alex.

The Role of AI and Team Changeability

AI can help teams better adapt to change by providing insights and recommendations that enable them to make more informed and effective decisions, applying this process to any disruptive change. AI can give teams a more comprehensive understanding of their environment, allowing them to anticipate better and respond to changes. For example, AI can analyze customer behavior and preferences, enabling teams to adjust their strategies and offerings in response to changing demand. AI can also analyze market conditions and trends, helping teams to identify new opportunities or potential risks. Additionally, AI can provide recommendations on the best course of action based on the analyzed data and insights. By providing these insights and advice, AI can help your team or teams make better decisions and adapt to change more quickly and effectively.

AI can foster collaboration and facilitate learning and development, enabling your team to stay ahead of the curve.

AI-powered collaboration tools can help team members communicate and share information more efficiently, regardless of location or time zone. This works well in a continued hybrid or remote work environment. These tools can also help teams to identify and resolve issues more quickly by automatically detecting patterns and anomalies in data and highlighting potential problems.

Employees value an investment in their development. AI can facilitate learning and development by providing personalized recommendations and training opportunities based on individual team members' strengths and weaknesses. Feedback and development plans can become more strategic. For example, AI can analyze employees' work patterns and suggest improving their productivity or efficiency. AI-powered training programs can also be tailored to each employee's needs and preferences, providing them with targeted learning experiences that help them to acquire new skills and stay up to date with the latest developments in their field.

By fostering collaboration and facilitating learning and development, AI can help teams stay ahead of the curve and adapt to changing circumstances more quickly and effectively. Companies will be more innovative and competitive and achieve their goals more efficiently and effectively.

AI Helps You to See What's Up Ahead

AI can identify emerging trends or potential risks in various contexts, enabling leaders to act quickly and proactively. Here are some examples:

Financial markets: AI can analyze large volumes of financial data to identify patterns and trends that may signal changes in the market, such as shifts in investor sentiment or the emergence of new market opportunities. This insight can help leaders to adjust their investment strategies or portfolio allocations in response to changing market conditions.

Supply chain management: AI can analyze supply chain data to identify potential bottlenecks or disruptions, such as delays in shipping or shortages of critical materials. This knowledge helps leaders to take action to address these issues before they become significant problems, such as by sourcing materials from alternative suppliers or adjusting production schedules.

Cybersecurity: AI can analyze network traffic and other security data to detect potential threats, such as malware or phishing attacks. Leaders can mitigate these threats before they result in data breaches or other security incidents.

Healthcare: AI can analyze patient data to identify potential health risks or trends, such as increases in certain illnesses or new diseases. This can help leaders to take action to prevent or mitigate these risks, such as by implementing new public health initiatives or investing in research and development.

The speed of change is only going to accelerate. AI can help you and your team be more agile and responsive to changes in your environment by providing real-time data and insights that enable them to make more informed and timely decisions: no more slow decision-making, siloed thinking, or lack of collaboration. Response to change will be quicker and laser-focused on what matters the most.

Coaching: I've introduced an AI Coach to our service delivery. Picture this: as you focus on growing, motivating, and developing your team, an AI app on your cell phone or in your Microsoft Teams meeting can provide instant feedback on your progress. It helps you prepare for meetings and offers immediate reports on your success in engaging and developing your team members. As you progress, it will measure your improvement. Your AI coach will guide you and provide unbiased feedback.

Ultimately, AI can enhance the coaching experience by delivering more personalized and actionable insights, allowing you to achieve your goals more quickly and effectively. AI is not a replacement for human coaches but can be a valuable tool to complement and enhance the coaching process.

Whether you want to improve your leadership skills, enhance your communication abilities, or develop new competencies, AI can provide the support and guidance you need to succeed.

As a leader, embracing new technologies like AI and leveraging them to your advantage is essential. By incorporating AI into professional development, you can enhance your effectiveness or that of your team, drive better results, and empower yourself and your team to reach new heights of success.

The Benefits of AI-Driven Adaptability and Agility in Action

Integrating artificial intelligence (AI) with change leadership, adaptability, and agility within the Changeability framework holds immense organizational potential. By harnessing AI, companies can unlock various benefits that increase operational efficiency, productivity, employee retention, engagement, and innovation.

Numerous companies have embraced AI to enhance their adaptability and agility, and their efforts have yielded remarkable results. Let's explore a few examples of what is possible:

1. An organization can gain real-time insights into market trends and customer preferences by implementing AI-powered analytics and machine learning algorithms. Product teams can adapt their product offerings swiftly, stay ahead of competitors, and meet the evolving demands of their target audience. How might AI-driven data analysis help your organization make informed decisions and respond rapidly to changing market dynamics?

2. Many companies have recognized the importance of enhancing employee engagement and talent retention by providing meaningful and transformative work opportunities. In this regard, AI-powered chatbots and virtual assistants have emerged as valuable assets. These intelligent tools play a pivotal role in streamlining internal communication, facilitating easy access to information,

and offering personalized support to employees. These AI-driven solutions empower organizations to create a more agile and adaptive workforce by automating repetitive and mundane tasks. Employees are freed from tedious administrative work, allowing them to redirect their time and energy toward strategic initiatives and innovative endeavors. This shift boosts productivity and nurtures a culture of creativity and collaboration, enabling employees to leverage their unique talents and skills to drive organizational growth.

3. Supply chains continue to be an ongoing concern. Organizations may implement AI-based predictive analytics to optimize supply chain and inventory management processes. The system generates accurate demand forecasts and recommended inventory levels in real-time by analyzing historical data, market trends, and external factors. This enables organizations to adapt their production and distribution strategies promptly, reducing waste, improving efficiency, and enhancing their agility in meeting customer demands.

4. Employee Effectiveness: AI can improve employee engagement and retention in several ways:

Personalization: AI can help personalize the employee experience by providing tailored learning and development opportunities, customized feedback, and personalized benefits and perks. By tailoring these experiences to individual employees, AI can help improve their engagement and satisfaction, ultimately reducing turnover.

Career Development: AI can also help employees identify career development opportunities and provide them with the tools and resources to achieve their goals. AI can help employees feel more invested in their careers and the company, ultimately improving their engagement and retention.

Predictive Analytics: AI can analyze employee data to identify patterns and insights to help predict which employees are at risk of leaving. Imagine being able to take proactive steps to retain these employees, such as offering new opportunities or increasing compensation.

Employee Wellness: AI can help improve employee wellness by analyzing data on employee health and well-being and providing recommendations for improvement. Data can include personalized wellness plans, access to mental health resources, and reminders to take breaks and prioritize self-care.

These examples illustrate the tangible benefits that AI-driven adaptability and agility can bring to organizations. By embracing AI technologies, companies can gain a competitive edge, proactively respond to industry shifts, and drive innovation. Change leaders and organizations need to explore how AI can be effectively integrated into their operations, aligning it with the principles of Changeability to unlock its full potential and drive sustained success.

Many companies have successfully leveraged AI to enhance their adaptability and agility, achieving significant results. Here are a few examples:

Amazon: Amazon has been a leader in using AI to improve its operations, including enhancing its supply chain management and logistics capabilities. The company uses AI to optimize delivery routes, manage inventory levels, and predict customer demand. By leveraging AI, Amazon has quickly adapted to changes in the market and customer preferences, enabling it to remain a dominant player in the e-commerce industry.

Cigna: Cigna is using AI to enhance the quality of care it provides to patients. In 2021, Cigna launched a clinical decision support system (CDSS) powered by AI to support its clinical teams in making more accurate and timely diagnoses. This system uses machine learning algorithms to analyze large amounts of patient data, such as medical histories, test results, and imaging data, to provide doctors with personalized treatment recommendations. The system analyzes patient data and generates real-time recommendations based on the patient's medical history and current symptoms.

By leveraging AI, healthcare companies can provide better patient care, reduce costs, and improve overall health outcomes. Additionally, AI can help healthcare providers to identify trends in patient health data that might otherwise go unnoticed, allowing them to take proactive steps to improve patient health and well-being.

Netflix: Netflix uses AI to personalize its content recommendations to individual users based on their viewing history and other data. These insights enable the company to provide a more tailored and engaging user experience, ultimately driving higher engagement and subscriber retention.

Zara: Zara, a global fashion retailer, uses AI to analyze customer data and identify emerging trends and preferences. The company leverages this data to design and produce new collections more quickly and efficiently, enabling it to stay ahead of the curve and remain competitive in the fast-paced fashion industry.

In each of these examples, AI has enabled companies to be more adaptable and agile by providing real-time data and insights that allow them to make more informed and timely decisions. As a result, these companies stay ahead of the curve and achieve significant results, such as improved operational efficiency, increased innovation, and higher customer engagement and retention.

How is your organization responding to AI? How well does it respond to disruptive technology change?

Sometimes it's best to get the conversation started by asking your team or organization a series of questions. Note "AI" could be replaced with any current technology disruption.

- What are our business goals, and how can AI help us achieve them?
- What are the benefits and drawbacks of using AI in our organization, and how can we mitigate potential risks?
- Do we have the data infrastructure and expertise to implement AI solutions effectively?
- How can we ensure that our AI algorithms are unbiased and ethical?
- How can we effectively integrate AI into our existing workflows and processes?
- What impact will AI have on our workforce, and how can we ensure our employees are prepared and trained to work with AI?
- How can we measure the impact of our AI initiatives and ensure they deliver value to our organization?

- What steps can we take to ensure we comply with relevant regulations and standards related to AI?
- How can we ensure that we are using AI responsibly and sustainably?

You can take these questions to your team or your next leadership meeting. By asking these and other critical questions, you can make informed decisions about using AI in your organization and ensure they leverage AI responsibly and effectively.

The Downside of AI

While AI-driven adaptability and agility have many benefits, some potential drawbacks and challenges must be considered.

Data Bias: AI relies on data to learn and make decisions, which means that if the data is biased or incomplete, the AI will produce biased or incomplete results. To overcome this, it is crucial to ensure that the data used to train the AI is diverse and representative of the population it is serving. Additionally, it is vital to continually monitor and audit AI to ensure that it is producing fair and unbiased results.

Ethical Concerns: AI has the potential to be used in unethical ways, such as invading privacy, reinforcing discrimination, or automating decisions that humans should make. To overcome this, establish ethical guidelines and regulations for AI development and deployment and ensure that AI is only used for ethical purposes.

Skill Gaps: Implementing AI requires specialized skills and knowledge, which can create skill gaps within organizations.

Organizations must invest in training and development programs to overcome this to ensure employees have the skills and knowledge necessary to work with AI.

Resistance to Change or Lack of Change Readiness: Some employees may resist change, particularly if AI is threatening their jobs or autonomy. To overcome this, involve employees in the implementation process and provide training and support to help them understand how AI will be used and how it can benefit them.

Cybersecurity Risks: AI can also pose cybersecurity risks, such as the potential for hackers to exploit vulnerabilities in AI algorithms or use AI to carry out cyber-attacks. To overcome this, it is essential to implement robust cybersecurity measures to protect systems and data.

AI can also be scary for some. Opening the conversation allows for discussion and promotes trust and psychological safety. Questions I've heard my clients ask include the following. "How will our jobs be impacted or enhanced? What do I need to learn? How will I stay relevant?" We help organizations to navigate the asked and unasked questions. Employees are worried, they wonder if they will be able to navigate the changes required by AI. Some will adapt quicker than others. We help leaders to understand which of their team members might be early adopters, who might need more training or support and who might meet change with resistance and require a bit more handholding. Understanding the complexity and personal needs of your team allows you to allocate resources and assign tasks effectively.

Overall, AI can be beneficial; however, one thing cannot be replaced, the human factor.

The Human Factor in an AI World

In the ever-evolving landscape of AI integration, it's crucial to acknowledge the unparalleled value of human relationships and intellect. As a leader of transformation and change, your role is pivotal in navigating the intersection of AI and organizational dynamics. While AI augments your leadership capabilities, it cannot replace the essence of human connection.

Human relationships are the bedrock of collaboration, empathy, and emotional intelligence, which are indispensable for driving successful transformations. While AI can enhance efficiency and decision-making processes, it's essential to recognize that human relationships and intellect remain paramount for fostering creativity, critical thinking, and ethical decision-making throughout the change journey.

Integrating AI into daily operations presents opportunities and challenges for organizations undergoing transformation. Investing in employee training and development programs ensures your team has the skills and knowledge to leverage AI effectively. By embracing AI technologies, organizations can achieve a competitive advantage by enhancing agility, adaptability, and responsiveness to environmental changes.

AI's transformative impact extends beyond organizational operations, reshaping the nature of work across various industries. Leaders of transformation who can adapt and stay ahead of the curve stand to capitalize on new opportunities, while those who fail to keep pace risk falling behind. You can confidently navigate uncertainty and drive sustainable success by embracing change leadership principles and leveraging AI to augment decision-making processes.

Incorporating AI into change leadership practices empowers teams to adapt and thrive in dynamic environments. AI tools provide valuable insights and recommendations, enabling teams to anticipate and respond to changes effectively. By fostering collaboration, breaking down silos, and promoting a data-driven culture, organizations can harness the full potential of AI to drive innovation and achieve strategic transformation goals.

As you lead your organization through the AI journey, consider leveraging AI as a tool for professional development, using mobile coaching apps to enhance leadership skills within your team. Educating yourself and your team about AI fundamentals and assessing AI opportunities within your organization are essential steps toward successful implementation. By cultivating an ethical and responsible approach to AI use, you can ensure transparency, fairness, and accountability in decision-making processes.

In conclusion, AI integration offers unprecedented opportunities for organizational transformation and innovation. By embracing the human factor alongside AI advancements, leaders of transformation can navigate change effectively and drive sustainable success in an AI-powered world.

You've explored the concepts of changeability and the essential skill sets, mindsets, and toolsets of change leadership, adaptability, and agility. But how do these concepts translate into real-world scenarios? The upcoming chapters connect the dots by discovering how to assess and cultivate your team's changeability, establish a culture primed for change, and put these principles into action, illustrated through a compelling case study. See firsthand how effective change leadership, adaptability, and agility can drive tangible business outcomes and foster professional growth within your organization.

CHAPTER 7

Evaluating Your
Team's Changeability:
A Path to Strengthening
Change Readiness

> *"It is not the strongest of the species that survives,*
> *nor the most intelligent. It is the one that is most*
> *adaptable to change."*
>
> **—Charles Darwin**

I've always liked the movie "Ford vs. Ferrari". In the exciting world of motorsports, where speed, precision, and innovation reign supreme, the film is an excellent example of Changeability. The iconic rivalry depicted in the movie "Ford vs. Ferrari" showcases the determination to win and offers profound lessons on adaptability and agility. Ferrari's dominance in the prestigious 24 Hours Le Mans, the 34th Grand Prix of Endurance in France, seemed unassailable. Ford, a giant in the automobile industry, sought to challenge Ferrari's reign and prove their prowess on the racetrack. It was a battle Henry Ford demanded to win, yet it seemed unattainable.

Race car legends Carroll Shelby (Matt Damon) and Ken Miles (Christian Bale) took on the challenge of building a car capable of winning. Miles sarcastically asked Shelby, "You're gonna build a car to beat Ferrari with a Ford?" Shelby replied, "Correct." Miles responded, "And how long did they tell you when they needed it? Two, three hundred years?" Shelby responded, "90 days."

Despite the seemingly impossible deadline, they gathered the best engineers to build a car that had never existed and would have the speed and endurance to surpass that of Ferrari. Not an easy feat.

The engineers used their well-honed knowledge to produce the GT-40, which would later become the Mustang, but the car had problems. The brakes would fail, and it had difficulty staying on the tarmac. Enticed by a recent engineering marvel—the computer—they installed one to collect data on vehicle performance to create computer models of the car's aerodynamic performance. Miles, who tended to be a bit more emotionally reactive and known to be "difficult" and not a "team player," came up with the solution. "It's not about speed to win the race. We need lightness and endurance to cater to the road." Henry Ford II told them they needed to "think like a Ferrari" to stay in business. So, they stepped away from what they knew and moved toward a more innovative solution.

They lightened the load and figured out what to optimize, let go of, and keep. They refined the aerodynamics to prevent the car from being pinned or lifted from the ground at high speeds. Once they designed the car, they knew the brakes would fail faster than other cars. Despite rules that question such a maneuver, they built the brake system to be replaced as a unit if needed quickly.

On the day of the race, they were ready. The long twenty-four-hour race kept the driver, the pit crew, Shelby, and the movie viewer focused through the intensity.

In the final scenes of "Ford vs. Ferrari," the culmination of the rivalry and grueling race unfolds. The Ford GT40, expertly driven by Ken Miles, showcases its exceptional performance and engineering, overtaking its competitors and leading the pack. Miles is poised to secure a historic victory for Ford as the finish line approaches. However, the story takes an unexpected turn as company politics and agendas come into play.

Curious as to what happened? If I told you, I'd spoil the movie.

When I partner with a team, I ask them to watch the movie and explore the themes they recognize within their organization. It also helps them to identify the framework of Changeability throughout:

Change leadership: The movie exemplifies the significant role of change leadership in fostering innovation and driving change. In particular, the visionary leadership of Carroll Shelby and Ken Miles played a pivotal role in enabling Ford to envision the ambitious goal of defeating Ferrari at the 24 Hours of Le Mans race, an achievement that had never been realized by an American automaker. Despite their contrasting personalities, Shelby and Miles united in their shared objective of winning. Shelby took charge of the customization of the winning car, developed the business case for the required resources, and effectively resolved conflicts as they arose.

Adaptability: The movie also highlights the importance of adaptability in a constantly changing environment. The characters in the film must adapt to changing circumstances, such as technological innovation and unforeseen obstacles, to achieve their goals. This serves as a reminder that adaptability builds the foundation for success.

Agility: Speed is critical in any race, and so is making wise data-informed choices. Ford had to pivot its strategy and approach to compete with Ferrari, and it was able to do so successfully thanks in part to its leadership and team agility. They solved problems together and at laser speed. The pit crew didn't change the oil when only tire rotation was required.

Overall, the story of "Ford v Ferrari" is a powerful example of the concepts explored in "Changeability." It is a story about courage, determination, and innovation. In addition, it portrays the human spirit of overcoming challenges and achieving greatness.

Now that you have honed your skills as a change leader, deepened your understanding of the essential skill sets, mindset, and environment required for your team to adapt to change, and explored ways to improve speed, scale, and responsiveness through agility, there is one crucial aspect that cannot be overlooked—building a team that is truly ready for change.

Think about a change currently taking place or soon to occur within your organization. What is needed to open the roadway to innovation?

First, make sure you are well-fueled. It is hard to see an opportunity or drive change if you feel depleted in energy. If you are overwhelmed by the number of projects ahead or find yourself questioning your team's ability to succeed it is hard to run the course.

One fundamental aspect to kickstart the innovation engine is ensuring you are adequately fueled. It can be challenging to spot opportunities and lead change when your energy levels are depleted. Self-care, mental fitness and physical health will keep your engine well-tuned. Your team needs to be ready and willing to win too but first, let's begin by looking at your team.

Revised Team Perspective

You might be excited about innovation and change or you might find time is too limited or there are too many competing priorities to even think of adding another.

If you ever find yourself overwhelmed by the multitude of impending projects or questioning your team's capacity to succeed, you're not alone.

That was the case with Randy, a Director charged with product development.

As an ambitious individual within his organization, he held a reputation as one of the most competent employees. Randy possessed a deep passion for his company and its future, brimming with innovative ideas. He strived to attend all meetings where key decisions were made. Yet coaching was suggested for Randy because while Randy moved full speed ahead, his team didn't always follow.

Every leader has their own "pit crew," a team relied upon to provide swift solutions and contribute their top-tier talent. Randy indeed had such a team, but he hadn't been looking at them through that lens.

As someone who consistently set high performance standards for himself, Randy often viewed his team as falling short in terms of competence. During our discussions, Randy shared insights into each of his team members and their respective roles within the organization. I asked questions about their strengths, areas for improvement, and the value they brought to the company. It became evident that Randy's emotional responses to each team member varied significantly. He held Susan in high regard, praising her consistent achievement of deadlines. However, when discussing Adam, Samantha, and Habeeb, a different narrative emerged. Randy tended to focus more on their perceived performance deficiencies and limitations, struggling to acknowledge their strengths. I knew that there was more to uncover beneath the surface.

Randy articulated his desire to use coaching to increase his visibility within the organization, aiming to establish himself as an expert in his field. His calendar was often saturated with back-to-back meetings, leaving him with insufficient time to expand his professional network and solidify his personal brand. On top of these meetings, Randy dedicated a significant portion of his week to supervising his team's work, ensuring accountability, and meticulously tracking project progress.

My priority was to focus on giving Randy back time, time to gain visibility, and to take his innovative ideas forward. I realized that for that to happen, Randy would need to trust his team. As part of our engagement, I interviewed his stakeholders, manager, peer, and team members. What I discovered didn't surprise me as I have heard it many times.

His manager believed Randy spent too much time "in the weeds" and couldn't attend decision-making meetings. His focus was siloed to his team versus that of the organization. They saw his potential and considered him a valued employee in the organization, yet for him to advance, he would need to figure out how to work differently with his team.

His peer was familiar with Randy but felt that she didn't know him well other than through project collaboration. She wasn't able to identify Randy's strengths and noted he often missed critical department-wide meetings.

Randy's team members respected his leadership and acknowledged his innovative ideas. However, they collectively expressed a desire for him to delegate more and grant them greater visibility for career advancement. They felt that Randy's tendency to micromanage occasionally created undue pressure, leading to occasional mistakes.

On the other hand, senior leadership held Randy's department in high regard, appreciating its stellar performance. Randy's expertise had earned him invitations to present at crucial meetings, meetings he often either couldn't attend or when attending or even when present, his message didn't effectively resonate. While his passion for his ideas shone through, his presentation style often led to confusion. Instead of conveying his thoughts in clear, business-oriented terms, he tended to focus on technical details, causing his messages to be less accessible to a broader audience. This approach led to situations where his proposals lacked proper context, leaving people uncertain about his focus and objectives. He left the meetings in despair, his big ideas cut on the conference room floor.

For Randy to meet his goals, it was evident that he needed to 1) develop and trust his team 2) delegate, allowing team members to attend his meetings 3) promote visibility for his team to facilitate their growth and advancement 4) adapt his communication style to engage others effectively, bridging the gap between technology and business terminology while inspiring others to embrace his innovative ideas.

However, that could only happen if Randy saw the potential in his team.

Consider your own team's competency. How would you rate their overall performance? Do you often find yourself wishing for more time to focus on your own priorities? Even among the highest-performing teams, it's not uncommon to encounter individuals who fail to reach their fullest potential. This can happen because they lack the opportunity to showcase their capabilities or because their leader already perceives them as having limitations.

How you "see" someone dictates how you feel about them, which then influences how you behave. Thoughts trigger feelings which trigger actions. Because Randy saw his team as underperforming, he labeled them incompetent and resisted allowing them to attend critical meetings.

Take a moment to reflect: how do you perceive your team members individually? Visualize each of them. Do you find yourself smiling when you think of some, while others evoke feelings of disappointment or frustration? Are your interactions with them influenced by the way you perceive them?

I once observed a restaurant manager reprimand her assistant manager, saying, "Mary set the table incorrectly again. We've already shown her how to do it, but she never seems to get anything right." The assistant manager gently reminded her that Mary was still new and learning. However, the manager had already formed the judgment that Mary was incapable and lacked the ability to improve. The phrase, "She will never learn," had already been etched in her mind.

What many leaders may not realize is that when you label individuals as incompetent, you inadvertently set yourself up to continually seek evidence of their failure and disappointment. Your perception can become a self-fulfilling prophecy, hindering their growth and potential.

To help Randy achieve his goals, we initiated a process that required him to reevaluate his perspective on his team. It all began with the development of an Engage and Mobilize plan. This plan involved a thorough review of each team member, with a focus on identifying and harnessing their individual strengths. As a part of this transformation, Randy began to assign small stretch assignments to his team members, which yielded surprising results—they were able to achieve their objectives without requiring his constant oversight.

To further optimize Randy's time management, we strategically assessed the meetings he attended. We started by identifying lower-risk meetings that he could delegate to his team, thereby reclaiming valuable hours in his schedule. To ensure the team's success in these meetings, I encouraged Randy to prepare them by providing insights into the personalities of the attendees and to clarify their role and the meeting's objectives. The key, I advised, was not to impose undue pressure or attempt to mold team members into miniature versions of himself.

Randy quickly observed his team members' competence in these meetings. They returned with enthusiasm and a readiness to address the agenda items at hand. This newfound efficiency allowed Randy to gradually carve out pockets of time in his schedule. With these gains in time management achieved, we shifted our focus to enhancing Randy's presentation skills and aligning his communication with the preferences and expectations of those present in the room.

Soon, Randy found himself with unallocated time in his calendar. At this juncture, I introduced what I've termed "W.O.M.B." time—a scheduled slot for "working on the business" rather than merely "in the business." Randy utilized this time to adopt a more strategic perspective of his department and the organization. He identified specific individuals with whom he wanted to establish connections, thereby building a robust network of relationships. He also had time to analyze current and projected trends, a process that yielded valuable insights.

Through diligent research and a proactive approach, Randy soon found himself being invited into meetings with senior leaders. Using his new skills in communication, he shared his innovative ideas regarding the company's products and their future trajectory. This initial recognition led to more meeting invitations, as Randy's thought leadership became increasingly valued.

Simultaneously, Randy's team members continued to excel in their roles, appreciating that he was providing greater exposure to the department's value and its potential contributions to the company's overall success. Within the span of a year, Randy's efforts earned him a promotion to Senior Director. He has since maintained his role as a catalyst for innovative business strategy and development.

I share this story because no one does this work alone. Use your talented team. They are your pit crew.

Randy's journey underscores a vital truth: many leaders I encounter underutilize their team's potential. They are not aware of the untapped capabilities until they take proactive steps to assess and unlock them. Through a process of assessment and gaining deeper insights into your team's composition, strengths, and abilities, you can unleash their collective potential. It's about seeing the possibilities within each team member, identifying latent talents waiting to be activated, and amplifying existing strengths.

When you do, every team member will take the lead, making critical decisions as needed and charting the course forward. In the realm of leadership, having a team who strives to win and is capable of initiating and leading change is the hallmark of a great leader.

How to Assess and Amplify Your Team's Change Readiness

As organizations evolve and market forces continue to shift, the ability to adapt and thrive in a changing environment is more important than ever. But how can you ensure your team is prepared to meet these challenges head on?

You probably know not all individuals respond to change similarly. So how do you know who on your team are your best leaders of change? Who on your team is the most innovative and creative? Who leads in ensuring everything complies with regulations and double-checks that wild ideas won't erode successful processes? Who has the grit to do what it takes to push on through, and who needs a slower pace or less time-critical aspects of your project?

One way to build this knowledge is to assess the change readiness of your team. Each individual and each team has different degrees of change readiness and ability to adapt and successfully implement change.

Identifying and Optimizing Your Team's Potential

Does your team leap into change because of their burning ambition or due to a burning platform? A Burning Platform is a metaphor used to explain the necessity of change despite the fear of the unknown consequences. This metaphor was derived from the fatal explosion of an oil drilling platform in which one survivor had to choose to jump into a sea of oil rather than burn on the platform. This metaphor serves to describe a situation in which action is required and maintenance of the status quo is no longer an option as doing so would be even more harmful. When facing a burning platform is your team ready to take the leap?

Change readiness refers to the level of preparedness and willingness of individuals and teams to embrace and navigate change. It involves having the necessary mindset, skills, and resources to adapt to new circumstances, overcome challenges, and seize opportunities presented by change. Change readiness is crucial in successful change implementation as it sets the foundation for a smooth transition and increases the chances of achieving desired outcomes.

Imagine a team meeting where everyone offers ideas, solutions for improvements, and innovation. Where problems are solved rapidly, and opportunities explored. How does this compare to the meetings you are experiencing?

When individuals and teams are change-ready, they are more open to new ideas, receptive to feedback, and willing to learn and develop new skills. They possess a positive attitude towards change, viewing it as an opportunity for growth and improvement rather than a threat. Change readiness helps foster a culture of adaptability, resilience, and essential continuous learning.

Factors Influencing Team's Readiness for Change

Team readiness for change is influenced by several factors, and these factors can vary depending on the specific organizational context, the nature of the change, and the dynamics within the team. Here are some common factors that play a crucial role in determining a team's readiness for change:

- Clear Communication: Effective and transparent communication about the change initiative is essential. When the purpose, goals, and expected outcomes of the change are clearly communicated, team members can better comprehend and align themselves with the change effort.

- Trust and Psychological Safety: The level of trust and psychological safety within the team significantly impacts readiness for change. Teams where members feel safe to express concerns, share ideas, and convey emotions without fear of judgment or negative consequences are more likely to be open and receptive to change.

- Leadership Support: The support and involvement of team leaders and managers are vital factors influencing readiness for change. When leaders actively advocate for the change, provide necessary resources and guidance, and demonstrate their commitment to the effort, it positively influences the team's readiness and willingness to embrace the change.

- Previous Change Experiences: Past experiences with change, whether positive or negative, can shape a team's readiness. Teams that have successfully undergone change initiatives in the past tend to be more open and adaptable to new changes. Conversely, teams that have encountered significant challenges or unsuccessful change attempts may exhibit higher levels of resistance or skepticism toward recent changes.

- Organizational Culture: The prevailing culture within the organization also plays a role. A culture that encourages innovation, learning, and adaptability can foster greater readiness for change among teams. In contrast, a culture that resists change or maintains rigid structures may hinder readiness.

- Alignment with Team Goals: The degree to which the change aligns with the team's goals and objectives can influence readiness. When team members perceive that the change supports their collective mission and vision, they are more likely to embrace it.

- Change Champions: Identifying and empowering change champions within the team can positively impact readiness. These individuals can serve as advocates and role models, helping to bridge the gap between the team and the change initiative.

- Change Management Practices: The quality of change management practices employed during the change process can affect readiness. Effective change management strategies, including planning, training, and addressing resistance, can enhance a team's preparedness for change.

The Role of Your Leadership in Fostering Change Readiness

Leadership plays a pivotal role in fostering change readiness within a team. Leaders set the tone, provide direction, and influence the team's attitudes and behaviors around change. Some key responsibilities of leaders in fostering change readiness include:

1. Creating a Compelling Vision: articulate a clear and compelling vision for the change, helping team members understand the purpose and benefits of the change initiative. This vision inspires and motivates team members to embrace change.
2. Effective Communication: communicate openly and transparently throughout the change process. Good meeting agendas include regular updates, addressing concerns, and actively listening to team members' feedback. Effective communication helps build trust, clarity, and commitment within the team.
3. Building Supportive Structures: establish supportive structures, processes, and resources that enable team members to navigate change successfully. Formats such as training, coaching, and mentorship opportunities develop the necessary skills and competencies for change.
4. Leading by example: embody the desired behaviors and attitudes that promote and support change. Leaders inspire team members to embrace change and develop the mindset required for successful implementation by demonstrating adaptability, resilience, and willingness to learn.
5. Encouraging Collaboration and Participation: Foster a collaborative environment where team members are actively involved in decision-making processes related to the change. Leaders create a sense of ownership and

empowerment by including team members in planning and implementation, enhancing change readiness.

In conclusion, leadership plays a crucial role in cultivating change readiness within a team. Effective leaders establish a clear and inspiring vision for change, communicate openly and transparently, and provide the necessary support structures to empower their team members. Leading by example, they embody the desired behaviors and attitudes that encourage adaptability and resilience. Furthermore, fostering collaboration and active participation among team members creates a sense of ownership and empowerment, ultimately enhancing the team's readiness for change. By taking on these responsibilities, leaders contribute significantly to the success of change initiatives and the overall adaptability of their teams.

Assessing Your Team's Change Readiness

What internal assessments do you use to assess your organization's creativity and readiness for innovation? Do you find them to be helpful?

Many client leaders I've worked with have expressed frustration with the limitations of traditional employee engagement and internal feedback surveys. While these surveys provide valuable information, they often fail to deliver actionable insights for driving meaningful transformation within their teams. That's where the power of the customized debrief from a comprehensive assessment comes in. Our assessment goes beyond surface-level data and deeply analyzes individuals' goals, competencies, and readiness for change.

Assessment plays a critical role in understanding and enhancing change readiness within your team. It provides valuable insights into the current state of your team's capabilities, identifies areas for improvement, and helps you tailor your strategies and resources to navigate and drive change effectively. One powerful tool in assessing change readiness is the AQ® Assessment.

You learned how individuals could use the AQ® Me assessment to understand and build their capacity for change.

The Adaptability Quotient (AQ® individual, team and organization) assessment is also available as a team assessment. In our Changeability Accelerator Initiative, we combine the assessment with a strategic leadership debrief, helping leaders to optimize their team's ability to:

The AQai® AQ® Assessment measures the Adaptability Quotient (A.Q.) of individuals and teams, comprehensively analyzing their readiness to embrace and thrive in the face of change. This assessment evaluates the critical components of change readiness, including mindset, skills, behaviors, and emotional intelligence. By using the AQai's AQ® Assessment, you gain a deeper understanding of your team's strengths and areas for development, enabling you to make informed decisions and take targeted actions to enhance their change readiness.

Leaders can leverage the results of the AQai® AQ® Assessment to gain valuable insights into their team's ability to navigate and drive change. By analyzing the assessment outcomes, you can identify the areas where your team excels or struggles, enabling you to allocate resources and support where they are most needed. This insight allows you to focus on building the necessary capabilities within your team, tailoring professional development plans to address individual needs, and fostering a culture of continuous learning and growth.

Moreover, the assessment results provide you with a roadmap to identify future leaders who possess the qualities to hire—those who embrace and conceive new ideas, pivot quickly, and drive the organization to meet its business objectives. By identifying individuals with high change readiness, you can nurture their leadership potential and empower them to spearhead change initiatives within your organization.

Assessment is crucial because it helps you make informed decisions and take targeted actions to enhance your team's change readiness. It guides you in identifying focus areas, allocating resources effectively, tailoring development plans, and identifying emerging leaders. By utilizing the AQai® AQ® Assessment, you can unlock the full potential of your team, foster a culture of change readiness, and propel your organization toward achieving its strategic objectives in a rapidly evolving business landscape.

I've worked with nearly three hundred team members and their leaders to optimize their teams over the past two years. The team analysis with strategic debriefing helped them understand how to improve engagement scores, identify the change potential in their team members, and build a viable strategic plan.

In my experience working with numerous organizations, I've observed a common challenge: while many organizations invest significant effort in identifying their core values or competencies, they often need an effective means to measure their success in achieving them through their employees. It's not enough to define these values or competencies; organizations need a robust measurement system to measure the impact and return on investment of these values. This measurement makes it easier to gauge the alignment between the organization's aspirations and employees' actual behaviors and actions. That's why implementing a reliable measurement framework is crucial to ensure that the organization's core values and competencies are not just empty words but deeply ingrained in the culture and reflected in the behaviors of every individual within the organization.

Regularly evaluating your team's change readiness using tools like the AQai® AQ® Team Assessment allows you to track progress, measure the impact of your interventions, and continuously adapt your strategies to meet your team's and organization's evolving needs.

So, embrace the power of assessment and equip yourself with the valuable insights it provides. By understanding your team's change readiness, you can confidently navigate and drive change and empower your team to thrive in dynamic environments.

My mission is to guide organizations through transformation and help them prepare for the future. The company name, "The Renegade Leader Coaching and Consulting Group," can evoke mixed reactions, especially from those deeply entrenched in the status quo and skeptical about the potential success of the future change. However, we also attract individuals and organizations who see the immense opportunity in embracing change and are eager to explore new possibilities. Regardless of where organizations fall on this spectrum, understanding their change readiness and reskill index level is crucial for establishing a baseline and determining the necessary steps for growth and development. Through a comprehensive assessment and coaching approach, we empower leaders and organizations to navigate change, unlock their full potential, and thrive in the dynamic business landscape of today and tomorrow.

The customized debrief session becomes a pivotal moment for leaders as they receive specific actions tailored to their team's needs. These actions range from quick wins to targeted development plans and even input into their existing strategies.

One client summed it perfectly when they said, "Finally, an assessment I can put to use." This feedback reflects the value of an assessment that provides information and translates it into practical actions that drive fundamental transformation and elevate employee engagement.

Assessment plays a critical role in understanding and enhancing change readiness within your team. It provides valuable insights into the current state of your team's capabilities, identifies areas for improvement, and helps you tailor your strategies and resources to navigate and drive change effectively. One powerful tool in assessing change readiness is the AQai® AQ® Assessment.

The AQ® Assessment measures the Adaptability Quotient (A.Q.) of individuals and teams, comprehensively analyzing their readiness to embrace and thrive in the face of change. This assessment evaluates the core components of change readiness, including mindset, skills, behaviors, and emotional intelligence. You gain a deeper understanding of your team's strengths and areas for development, enabling you to make informed decisions and take targeted actions to enhance their change readiness.

Leaders can leverage the results of the AQai® AQ® Assessment to gain valuable insights into their team's ability to navigate and drive change. By analyzing the assessment outcomes, you can identify the areas where your team excels or struggles, enabling you to allocate resources and support where they are most needed. This insight allows you to focus on building the necessary capabilities within your team, tailoring professional development plans to address individual needs, and fostering a culture of continuous learning and growth.

Remember, assessment is not a one-time event but an ongoing process. Regularly evaluating your team's change readiness using tools like the AQai® AQ® Assessment allows you to track progress, measure the impact of your interventions, and continuously adapt your strategies to meet your team's and organizations evolving needs.

So, embrace the power of assessment and equip yourself with the valuable insights it provides. By understanding your team's change readiness, you can confidently navigate and drive change, empower your team to thrive in dynamic environments, and propel your organization toward sustained success.

Imagine learning your team's capacity for change. Does your team score high on exploring and transforming or utilizing and improving, or are they balanced? Which is better? It depends on your business and the goals you are trying to achieve. One heavily compliant regulatory team means to focus on incremental improvements. Others may be maximizing their potential and are focused on innovation. I've also seen where teams are supposed to be innovating yet are hardly scoring in utilizing and improving, meaning there is little time for creativity. I've also seen team members with high scoring on exploring and transformation leave jobs that don't ignite their passion for creativity.

Are you focused on implementing a new internal process or competency? What teams will be your early adopters and who might have more significant training requirements?

Throughout this book, you have honed your skills, delved into the mindset and skill sets required for change, and explored the power of agility in driving success. As you've discovered, change leadership is a collaborative endeavor. It requires a team ready and equipped to adapt, embrace change, and drive transformation.

Remember, the success of change initiatives lies not only

in your leadership capabilities but also in your team's collective efforts and readiness. Empowering your team with the tools and mindset to embrace change will pave the way for sustainable growth, innovation, and success.

The upcoming chapter focuses on assessing and amplifying an organization's change readiness. We will explore how to evaluate the preparedness of different departments, teams, and organizational stakeholders. By determining collective readiness, you can identify potential gaps, strengths, and areas for improvement that span beyond individual teams.

Understanding the organization's change readiness is essential for leaders and change agents to make informed decisions and develop tailored strategies that address systemic challenges. We will uncover assessment techniques, tools, and methodologies designed explicitly for organizational change readiness.

Moreover, we will discuss how to interpret the assessment results and develop actionable plans to amplify the organization's change readiness. Building upon the foundation established by team readiness, we will explore strategies to align departments, foster collaboration, and enhance organizational capabilities to embrace and thrive in a changing environment.

Focusing on organizational change readiness can effectively mobilize the organization toward successful implementation. Through a collective effort, we can foster a culture of adaptability, resilience, and continuous improvement that permeates every aspect of the organization.

CHAPTER 8

Empowering Organizational Change Readiness

> *If you can't fly, then run. If you can't run, then walk. If you can't walk, then crawl. But whatever you do, you have to keep moving forward"*
> —**Martin Luther King Jr.**

Imagine completing a feat that generally would have taken years in only sixty hours. Yet that is precisely what the Cianbro, a Portland Maine company was able to do. The Portland construction crew achieved an extraordinary innovation by replacing an interstate 295 bridge, one of the busiest roads in the state carrying upwards to 53,000 vehicles a day, in one weekend.

You've likely experienced the frustration of traffic delays caused by construction or the uncertainty of following detour signs, wondering if they will lead you to your desired destination on time. It can't be enjoyable when it disrupts your daily commute or plans for essential events. Rerouting traffic wasn't even considered an option by this innovative firm.

Instead, the structurally deficient sixty-one-year-old bridge was disassembled and replaced by ninety person teams working around the clock in twelve-hour shifts. The new 80-foot long, 47-foot wide and nearly 400-ton bridge halves, constructed nearby, were then maneuvered into place, the approaches graded and paved. All work was completed in time for commuters to use it without weekday delay thanks to the coordination, innovation, and collaboration of Cianbro, Shaw Brother and HNTB Corporation.

Just imagine the remarkable capabilities, confidence, and collaboration required to achieve such an extraordinary result. Could it be because Cianbro's core values revolve around innovation, efficiency, environmental sensitivity, and their unwavering can-do spirit? Or their collaborating firm's dedication to putting people first, employees, customers, and community? Or the fact that all three organizations focused on "people first" and created a culture where ideas are heard, and all voices are valued?

All three organizations share a strong foundation built upon dedication, respect, and innovation. Their employees embrace an "owner's mindset," creating a culture that fosters psychological safety for idea-sharing. Leaders within these organizations model collaboration, creativity, and out-of-the-box thinking.

The teams possessed the mindset to challenge the status quo, question conventional wisdom, and explore uncharted territories of innovation and efficiency. Instead of accepting that bridge replacements are inevitably lengthy and challenging, they dared to envision a different reality. Leveraging their collective expertise, they pushed the boundaries of what was possible and crafted an ingenious plan.

I can't seem to get this example out of my mind. How did these three organizations envision something that wasn't done before?

Embracing Possibility

Imagine yourself getting into a helicopter and feeling the roundness of the seat as you hover above your office building. You see the rooftop and through it, you are able to see the bustling activities below. From this elevated viewpoint, you witness the daily operations, the interactions between departments, and the relationships with customers. You observe the engagement and happiness of your team members, the collaboration or lack thereof, and the leadership dynamics within the organization.

As you take in this panoramic view, you notice patterns and insights. You see the areas where your team excels, effortlessly tackling tasks and achieving remarkable results. At the same time, you recognize the challenges they face, the places where they may feel overwhelmed or underutilized. You become aware of the growth potential, both individually and collectively, and the untapped possibilities waiting to be explored.

Looking at the interactions between departments, you gauge the level of cooperation and alignment. Are they seamlessly working together, driven by shared values and a common purpose? Or do you sense a need for synergy to be improved? Recognizing the importance of fostering a supportive and accountable environment, you contemplate ways to strengthen these connections and drive collective success.

Beyond the organization's walls, you cast your gaze toward your customers. Their satisfaction and engagement become evident, and you reflect on your organization's impact on their lives. Are they genuinely delighted with the products and services you provide? Are they experiencing the value and support they seek? These questions prompt you to consider enhancing the customer experience and deepening those relationships.

Finally, you turn your attention to the leadership offices. You envision the leaders who steer the organization's course. Do they operate as a cohesive team united by a shared vision and a drive for innovation? Are they championing new ideas and inspiring others to think outside the box? As you ponder these dynamics, you recognize the potential for fostering stronger relationships and collaboration with these leaders.

As you descend from the helicopter, the fresh perspective from this bird's-eye view lingers in your mind. You've recognized strengths, and you might know what needs to change.

Returning to your office, you sit back in your chair, feeling a renewed sense of possibility and excitement. You understand that the organization has the power to transcend its current state and strive for distinction. Do you see what is possible?

Armed with this new knowledge and perspective, you

are poised to guide your organization towards organizational distinction, igniting changeability and unleashing the untapped potential within. Take a moment to note what you know to be possible.

I've entered the halls of organizations and felt the lack of innovation. People pass the threshold without a smile or a hello to other employees—conference rooms with silent voices other than those at the end of the table. I've been on Zoom kick-off calls looking only at the smiling face of my assistant as all others had their screens off, their names showing in small white print within their square. The organization gave them permission to no longer share their camera.

In contrast, I've also seen the Zoom faces come to life, the buzz of engagement in the hallways, and people standing in the conference room all working together at the whiteboard. All organizations have the potential to "come alive."

What do you think is needed for your organization to rise to distinction?

In the movie "Ford vs. Ferrari," you read about the power of leadership, creativity, and innovation in the face of intense competition. Similarly, cultivating a culture of changeability is crucial for driving success in the realm of organizational change. It requires embracing change leadership, adaptability, and agility as critical components of your organization's DNA.

Creating a culture of changeability requires a holistic approach. It starts with recognizing the symptoms of reduced change readiness, such as resistance to change, low innovation, poor communication, lack of accountability and engagement, and a general lack of support for change initiatives. By addressing these symptoms head-on, you can begin the transformation towards organizational change distinction.

By fostering a culture of flexibility, adaptability, innovation, and continuous improvement, your organization can pivot and adjust its strategies, processes, and structures. You also create internal systems that are lean, flexible, and scalable. It empowers your organization to adapt and evolve in the face of new circumstances continuously.

The good news is we can now assess the environmental factors that determine an organization's ability to thrive during times of change and, like your team, its change readiness for the future.

In the last chapter, you read how to assess and amplify your team's change readiness. Now, turn your focus towards the broader perspective of determining your organization's readiness. While understanding the willingness of individual teams is vital, assessing the organization's overall readiness provides a comprehensive view of its capacity to navigate change successfully.

You learned about the Adaptability Quotient (AQ®) ten dimensions, an ability which measures the degree of adaptability (grit, mental flexibility, mindset, resilience, and unlearning), and of character, who adapts and why they adapt which includes the dimensions of emotional range and regulation, extraversion, hope, motivation style, and thinking style.

The last five dimensions of adaptability are specific to the work environment and contain the sub-dimensions that influence people's ability to adapt, the degree of company support, team support, emotional health, work stress, and their work environment.

As you read through each of the dimensions, ask yourself, do you have a work culture that fosters an environment that supports or minimizes innovation?

When you assess your organizational Changeability, you gain insight into the five dimensions of adaptability and your company's unique results across teams, departments or organization wide.

Company Support: Company Support refers to the general perceptions employees have around the extent to which their organization values their contribution and cares about their well-being.

What makes you feel like your organization supports you?

Low company support is indicated by a lack of belongingness. A focus that many Diversity, Equity, and Inclusion initiatives try to improve. During times of change employees may feel that the organization is uncaring or distant. During the pandemic I am sure there were many times when, despite all their efforts, some employees felt isolated and wondered if the organization cared about their well-being. Lack of company support also contributes to erosion of emotional well-being and mental health. As a result, these employees become less committed, especially during times of change.

Medium scores in company support indicate a questioning if there is a spark or connection to their organization. They may feel there is a lack of integrity or genuineness in the care their company displays. They question its value. In contrast, high company support scores indicate a mutual sense of loyalty. The employee feels valued and is less likely to leave. With retention concerns and organizations losing top talent it is wise to strive to increase employees' perception of their company's support.

There are ways to increase employees' view of their organization.

- Provide the resources, assistance, and encouragement needed to help them perform their job duties effectively and achieve their personal and professional goals.

- Offer training and development opportunities to help employees build skills and advance in their careers.
- Give encouraging, supportive and constructive feedback on their performance.
- Offer a growth trajectory and be actively involved in committing time to its support.
- Recognition and rewards for their achievements and contributions to the company.
- Deliver flexible work arrangements and policies that support work-life balance and well-being.

According to a survey by the Society for Human Resource Management (SHRM), seventy-two percent of employees rated "respectful treatment of all employees at all levels" as the top factor in job satisfaction. The same SHRM survey found that sixty-four percent of employees rated "trust between employees and senior management" as important to job satisfaction.

Employees who generally perceive that their organization cares about their contribution and well-being have higher degrees of loyalty and engagement. They go further and are less likely to leave an organization, even in turbulent times.

The second dimension of Environment is Team Support. How freely do you feel you can share new knowledge, ideas and opinions, positive or negative, at work?

Team Support refers to the team environment in which employees feel they can share their new knowledge, share their opinion and are supported through challenges.

Low team support is reflected when employees feel they must "keep their head down and do the work in front of you." During times of change teams become competitive, there is less sharing of ideas, members feel rejected by others and there is less risk taking and problem solving.

Medium scores reflect team members feeling aligned with a close-knit group within the team. They still are cautious in sharing ideas with a broader audience and promote only lower risk options.

Increase team support by:

1. Encouraging diverse thought, allowing for all ideas to be respectfully heard.
2. Offer stretch assignments that allow team members to get to know other team members better and to work in collaboration.
3. Build opportunities for social interactions and unfocused chats to build trust throughout the team.

If employees do not feel supported by their team, they may experience a range of adverse outcomes that can ultimately impact their job satisfaction, performance, and overall well-being. Team support has the highest correlation to a positive predictor of organizational ability to innovate, accelerate change, and maximize employee performance and engagement.

A study by the Society for Human Resource Management found that employees who feel supported by their team members are sixty seven percent more engaged in their work. (Source: Society for Human Resource Management, *Creating a Culture of Supportive Coworkers*) According to a study by Glassdoor, companies with high levels of employee satisfaction and support outperformed the S&P 500 by one hundred and twenty-two percent over ten years. (Source: Glassdoor, *Top 50 Best Places to Work*, 2021)

The third component of the Environment pertains to the Work Environment. What changes in your environment would reduce stress levels? What resources would these changes require and how might they be justified?

Work Environment is about something other than desks and chairs. It is defined as the systems and methodologies in place in an employee's environment, not the physical workplace. Does the work environment encourage disruption, rapid experimentation and regular adaptation or does it restrict or hamper them?

Low scores are reflective of a close or pragmatic environment. Employees might fear negative outcomes, hide mistakes, feel afraid and avoid sharing ideas.

A medium score is tentative, the employee may struggle amongst ineffective processes and feel ideas are stifled by the organization or experience blockages to progress.

"As a physician, I can diagnose and provide solutions in 15 minutes or less. I see solutions to problems all the time. In my healthcare organization, there is nowhere to go with an innovative idea. If they hear it, they want you to run with it, and who has the time to go it alone?" a client once said. This is an example of a work environment concern.

High scores indicate an open and experimental environment. People feel rewarded for sharing new ideas. They have confidence in trying new practices, even if failing forward. Mistakes are openly shared, and creative thinking is encouraged.

To improve work environment:

- Give opportunity for experimentation even within the guardrails of compliance or regulation.
- Encourage innovation.

- Celebrate failures as learning experiences.
- Model a growth mindset and learning agility.

The fourth dimension of Environment, Work Stress, often contributes to an erosion of emotional health and well-being, leads to lower productivity, mistakes, rework and absenteeism. How well do you recognize when work stress has increased for yourself or your team? What would help to relieve it? How might you make that happen?

Work Stress is the sense of overwork and the feeling of overwhelm in your organization. It is something I hear about quite often from most employees and is in place but less openly admitted by the leaders I work with. Some stress is needed, like a rubber band, we all need some stretch and stepping into new areas outside of the comfort zone can be stressful yet innovative.

Low work stress means the individual feels they can handle their workload with ease. They have the capacity for their tasks and can finish.

Medium work stress allows for some time for experimentation, yet they also have moments of overwhelm.

High work stress indicates the employee has too much for one person to do. Often this is reported by the teams and departments I partner with as well. They are unable to complete daily tasks, always fall behind and are too stressed to try new things. This can easily lead to burnout.

Some ways to minimize stress is to:

- Inventory: make a list of stressors you or your team are experiencing. What can be minimized?
- Discuss habits you or the team could put in place to reduce work stress.

- Take time to prioritize work and to shift tasks as needed when new assignments arrive.
- Have open discussions about the workload and redistribute it, if possible, within the team.

Today I read my client organization's glossy 2021-2023 strategic plan. Big goals, breakthroughs, innovation, and strategic alignment with future trends. Exciting. The same organization completed our Adaptability Assessment focused on change Ability, Character, and Environment with predictive change readiness and reskill indexes. 52% are experiencing high stress, and 29% are neutral, experiencing healthy stress that moves productivity forward however are on the cusp of burnout if not given time to recuperate and re-energize. With only 19% of employees reporting low stress, will the well-formed strategic plan be successfully executed?

According to a survey by the American Institute of Stress, 80% of workers feel stress, and 40% say their job is very stressful. According to the American Institute of Stress, 83% of US workers suffer from work-related stress, with 25% saying their job is the number one stressor in their lives.

Depression-induced absenteeism costs US businesses $51 billion a year. Employees indicate the leading causes of workplace stress are workload (39% of workers), interpersonal issues (31%), juggling work and personal life (19%), and job security (6%).

Work stress and the last Environment dimension, Emotional Health are ones not to be ignored.

Emotional Health refers to the degree to which individuals are thriving at work, by experiencing positive moments while limiting negative ones. Think about a negative event you experienced. Write the words to describe it. Now reframe the same event with positivity. Do you feel the shift in the reframe?

Low emotional health projects a negative perception of change. Work is stressful, they feel bogged down and nervous about taking on anything more.

Medium individuals are not bothered by change or their environment, they are calm even within negativity yet they still feel stuck and weary of added change.

High emotional health scores indicate excitement about change, they welcome nuances with relaxed emotions and feel supported emotionally by their environment.

To improve emotional health:

- Create positive moments even during times of negativity.
- Reduce gossip and toxicity in the workplace by countering it with learned optimism.
- Discover ways to manage stress and celebrate positive attitudes.

In a study by Deloitte, 77% of workers said that they had experienced burnout at their current job, and 84% believed that burnout was a workplace issue. These statistics suggest that emotional health in the workplace is an essential issue that employers should address to support their employees and maintain a productive workforce. Good emotional health can be necessary for a person's ability to navigate change effectively. People who are emotionally healthy are better equipped to manage stress, cope with uncertainty, and adapt to new situations.

For example, an emotionally healthy person may be more resilient in the face of change and able to maintain a positive outlook. They may be better able to communicate their needs and concerns, work collaboratively with others, and maintain a sense of purpose and direction during times of transition.

Having assessed the work environment of nearly three hundred employees in the past few months, we found pockets of elevated levels of work stress, a reduction in the sense of team support which flows into the perception of company support, and an erosion of the work environment and resulting emotional health. We were able to debrief the leadership and laser focus on quick interventions. With others, we provide a postmortem; between the assessment and when we met with administration, fifty percent of one team had already left, several without other jobs to go to. Lack of team support, company support and high work stress were key contributors.

This was not within an uncaring organization. Instead, I find many organizations are blind to the root causes that slow them down and, without intervention, stifle their growth and ultimate success. Other organizations score low in overall change readiness; their teams are less equipped to navigate or initiate change; this, too, leaves them at risk for slow growth or, worse, extinction.

By embracing change leadership, adaptability, and agility, you can shift your organization. You can create a culture where innovation thrives, collaboration knows no bounds, and individuals feel empowered to contribute their unique talents and perspectives.

First, ask if the current assessment and data gathering provides the insights needed to impact your Adaptability environment outcomes. Do they provide you with the actionable insights you need? As you might see, the ROI of correcting environmental factors might be worth the risk to improve employee engagement, attrition, learning and development, and change readiness.

If you don't have the data in-house, consider an Organization Changeability Assessment, which includes the adaptability scores across individuals, teams, and the organization, with the opportunity to filter to refine results through demographics, job titles, and tenure, deepening your insight. We provide an actionable debrief customized to your goals and business outcomes.

High-performing organizations can innovate, gain efficiency and deliver on their business promises. Benefits include:

1. Enhanced Strategic Decision-Making: Knowing the change readiness score provides valuable insights into the organization's overall preparedness for change. This information enables leaders to make more informed and strategic decisions regarding change initiatives' timing, scope, and magnitude. They can align resources, adjust timelines, and tailor change management approaches to match the organization's readiness.

2. Targeted Development Efforts: Understanding the reskill index helps identify specific areas where the organization may need to develop or enhance skills and competencies. This knowledge allows leaders to focus training and development efforts on the most critical areas, ensuring employees have the skills to adapt to changing demands and seize new opportunities. Targeted development initiatives lead to a more agile and capable workforce.

3. Improved Change Implementation: With the change readiness score, organizations can proactively address potential barriers and resistance to change. They can design effective communication strategies, build support networks, and implement change management interventions that cater to the organization's specific readiness level. This proactive approach increases the

likelihood of successful change implementation, reduces disruption, and minimizes employee resistance.

4. Enhanced Agility and Adaptability: Knowing the reskill index helps organizations identify skill gaps and areas where they may need to catch up in the rapidly evolving business landscape. Organizations can foster a culture of continuous learning, adaptability, and innovation by prioritizing reskilling efforts. This emphasis on skill development enables the organization to respond swiftly to market changes, embrace emerging technologies, and stay competitive in a dynamic environment.

5. Increased Employee Engagement and Satisfaction: When employees perceive that the organization is invested in their development and growth, it enhances their sense of value and engagement. Understanding the change readiness score and reskill index demonstrates the organization's commitment to supporting employees through change. This commitment fosters a positive work environment, increases job satisfaction, and encourages employee loyalty.

6. Positive Organizational Culture: Assessing change readiness and reskill index promotes a culture of transparency, continuous improvement, and proactive change management. It signals to employees that the organization values their input, encourages personal growth, and embraces change as an opportunity for progress. This positive organizational culture cultivates resilience, innovation, and collaboration, which are crucial for long-term success.

173

Instilling Changeability: The Key to Your Organization's Success:

Teams are vital in driving change within organizations, but the ability to adapt and innovate should extend beyond individual teams. True transformation requires a holistic approach that encompasses your entire organization. By shifting your focus from teams to organizational change readiness and innovation, you can unlock your organization's full potential and achieve sustainable success in constant change.

Benefits of Changeability for Your Organization: By embracing changeability and prioritizing organizational change readiness and innovation, your organization can enjoy numerous benefits. These include:

1. Enhanced Agility and Adaptability: Changeability equips your organization with the agility and adaptability needed to respond effectively to market shifts, technological advancements, and customer demands. It enables your organization to pivot quickly, seize opportunities, and stay ahead of the competition.

2. Increased Innovation and Creativity: A culture of changeability fosters an environment where innovation and creativity thrive. By empowering your employees to think outside the box, challenge the status quo, and explore new ideas, your organization can drive innovation, generate fresh perspectives, and bring about breakthrough solutions.

3. Improved Change Management: When prioritizing change readiness, your organization is better equipped to manage and navigate organizational transformations. You have the structures, processes, and mindset

to minimize resistance, overcome obstacles, and successfully implement change initiatives.

4. Heightened Employee Engagement and Satisfaction: Changeability creates an environment where your employees feel valued, engaged, and supported. When individuals are empowered to contribute their unique skills and perspectives, they experience a sense of fulfillment and job satisfaction. This, in turn, leads to higher employee retention rates, increased productivity, and a positive organizational culture.

To truly understand and enhance your organization's change readiness and innovation capabilities, it is crucial to have a comprehensive assessment tool. The Organization AQ® Assessment is a powerful tool designed to measure your organization's readiness for change and ability to drive innovation. This assessment provides valuable insights into your organization's strengths, weaknesses, and areas for improvement, serving as a roadmap for transformation.

Fast Forward Actions:

- Assess Your Organization's Environment: Take the AQ® Organizational Assessment to evaluate your organization's adaptability and the health of its work environment. This assessment can provide valuable insights into the current state of your organization's culture and areas that need improvement.
- Engage in Leadership Development: Invest in leadership development programs that empower your leaders to foster a positive work culture. Equip them with the skills

and knowledge to lead change initiatives effectively and inspire their teams to embrace change.

- Promote Open Communication: Encourage open and transparent communication within your organization. Create channels for employees to share feedback, voice concerns, and contribute to decision-making processes. Effective communication is key to building a healthy work environment.

- Cultivate a Culture of Inclusivity: Prioritize diversity and inclusion in your organization. Ensure that all voices are heard and that employees from diverse backgrounds feel valued and included. Inclusivity fosters innovation and a more dynamic work culture.

- Continuous Improvement: Commit to continuous improvement in your organizational culture. Regularly review and update your policies, practices, and programs to align with your desired work environment. Listen to employee feedback and be willing to adapt as needed.

By taking these forward actions, you can contribute to building a great work environment and culture within your organization, which, in turn, will enhance your ability to navigate and thrive in times of change.

As you embark on the journey of organizational transformation, assessing and amplifying your organization's change readiness and innovation capabilities is crucial. By shifting the focus from teams to organizational change readiness, you unlock your organization's full potential, achieve sustainable success, and thrive in uncertainty. The Organization AQ® Assessment is a valuable tool to assess and to make informed decisions, tailor development plans, and embark on a transformative journey toward organizational excellence. Take advantage of this opportunity to unleash your organization's changeability and drive meaningful and impactful transformations.

Now that you understand the importance of changeability and its benefits to organizations, it's time to delve into a real-life story of a team and organization that wholeheartedly embraced changeability. This inspiring tale will showcase how their commitment to change readiness and innovation led to remarkable outcomes and transformative growth.

In this next chapter, you will witness the journey of a team that recognized the power of changeability and embarked on a path of transformation. As they embraced new mindsets, developed essential competencies, and fostered a culture of innovation, the team members experienced personal and professional growth in every aspect measured. Their dedication to change readiness paid off not only in their development but also in elevated customer satisfaction scores, reflecting their ability to adapt and deliver exceptional results. Additionally, the team's engagement skyrocketed, achieving a remarkable 162% increase—an undeniable testament to the positive impact of changeability.

This captivating story will give you insights into the specific strategies, practices, and mindset shifts that propelled this team and organization to new heights. You will discover the possible tangible benefits when you embrace changeability and cultivate a culture of innovation.

CHAPTER 9

A Case Study in Changeability, Adaptability, and Innovation

"Every success story is a tale of constant adaptation, revision and change."
            —Richard Branson

Introduction:

T he following case study in Changeability could take place in any industry, technology, healthcare, finance, your industry. It could be any size company from start-ups to worldwide enterprises. It could be your organization. Within any business stands a customer. The reason why the business exists. My client's customers range from internal customers to corporate giants like Boeing, Exxon, Shell, and Microsoft. This story could relate to any team, any department. Your team. As you read, I invite you to imagine your organization, your customer, your team.

The Client:

The Rockland Organization (fictional name) is well established. Its name and reputation would be known to most businesses within the United States and most likely worldwide. It is committed to excellence, growth, stability, and innovation. It balances the tightrope of exploration and creativity within the guardrails of regulation. It also longingly looks over the edge to what else might be possible for its organization and for its people to grow, to optimize customer excellence and to maximize its impact within its industry.

Rockland's core values include:

- **Customer-Centric Excellence**: To become a trusted partner, prioritize listening to customers, empathizing with their needs, and offering a compelling perspective.
- **Care and Understanding**: Cultivate a culture of care for one another and our communities, marked by humility, kindness, genuine connections, and unwavering commitment to collaboration.

- **Inclusive Belonging**: Embed diversity and inclusion in every decision to foster a welcoming environment for diverse voices, fresh perspectives, and innovative potential.
- **Growth-Oriented Mindset**: Embrace stepping out of your comfort zone, learning from both failures and successes, and avoiding the trap of a fixed mindset.
- **Ownership Mentality**: Show up with excellence, take accountability, and act swiftly and with integrity, embodying the sense of ownership required to shape the future.

To develop their people, the company aligned with the Korn Ferry's leadership competencies condensed into key domains:

1. **Thought Leadership**: This domain focuses on intellectual agility, strategic thinking, and innovation.
2. **Results Leadership**: It emphasizes the ability to drive results, manage execution, and demonstrate financial acumen.
3. **People Leadership**: This domain centers on interpersonal skills, collaboration, and talent development.
4. **Personal Leadership**: It highlights self-awareness, resilience, and adaptability as essential leadership qualities.

Organizational Priorities:

The organization had several priorities, a few of which were:

- Innovation and Growth
- Risk Intelligence
- Diversity, Equity, Belonging and Inclusion

- Talent Management, Retention and Development
- Digital Transformation

People Development:

With a focus on their core values, desired competencies and priorities, Rockland sought resources to build a strong foundation of confidence, competency, and capacity within their teams. That is when my company, The Renegade Leader Coaching and Consulting Group, was hired.

Change Intelligence: Building the Capacity for Change:

Rockland, like most companies, was in a constant state of change. Technology changes, changes in leadership, customer demands, and business expectations topped their list. Their highly skilled technology team was trained in change management. They now wanted to build change capacity in their employees.

We started with a change leadership assessment to identify leadership styles, to understand how to communicate effectively across styles and how to adapt to differences.

We focused on the head, heart and hands of change leadership. The heart connects people to the change being made, the head enrolls people into the big vision and offers an understanding of why change is needed, and hands offer the tools and resources needed to execute the change. Resistance is caused when people lack buy-in to the change, don't understand its value or are unsure of their role and responsibility in the change. This model aligned well with their Prosci ADAR model for change, building awareness, desire, knowledge, ability, and reinforcement.

Insight Gained:

This organization weighed heavily in head and hands. They often articulated their vision for change and built the roadmap to execute, however, they scored lower in heart, effectively communicating, engaging, and inspiring others during times of change. This gap often slowed them down, resulting in miscommunication, misaligned priorities and the risk of minimizing the financial and efficiency benefits of the change.

Teams left with a clear understanding of the difference between being a visionary of change versus a driver, champion, and other change leadership avatars. The assessment was followed by a two-hour training focused on the specific change impact within each department and attendees left with greater awareness of their team, ways to bridge differences and an action plan to execute on their change.

Building the skills and capacity for change would shortly become their foundation for managing change.

Adaptability Intelligence: Transforming Adaptability to Change

Rockland understood the value of investing in a development tool that would accelerate innovation, reduce employee burnout, improve well-being, and unlock team performance, strengthening their entire organizations' relationship with change. They liked that the assessment and training provided was based on scientific data and research and provided predictable improvements when focusing on the right levers of change. When we presented an overview of Adaptability Intelligence the organization quickly saw how it aligned with their priorities, their core values, and their competencies.

They were ready to reskill and upskill employees to produce faster results across the organization.

We began with an assessment of three hundred individuals. The assessment measured individual ability in times of change, their grit, mindset, mental flexibility, resilience, and ability to unlearn to learn new ways of working. In addition, it outlined their character preferences, emotional range, reactive or steadiness, extraversion, their degree of hope, motivation, and their thinking style. Lasty, it measured their perception of their environment, company support, team support, work environment and degree of work stress, all attributes which can contribute to or hinder change. In addition, they received a score in their tendency to prefer to explore and transform or utilize and improve.

We then grouped those individuals by team, providing team leaders with key insights about their team and strategies for quick wins and key strategies related to their department priorities. Our recommendations were specific to their goals. The science and data give my team insight into which levers to utilize to maximize specific improvements. For example, the dimensions that apply to a successful digital transformation are different from those for increasing risk intelligence.

We then looked at each department and compared the other departments. Which departments would best be leveraged in times of organization wide change? Lastly, we reviewed the organization. Given the results, how successful might they be in meeting their core objectives? What areas of Ability, Character or Environment would create obstacles and what opportunities could they use to mitigate? Through executive debriefs with department leaders and the senior leadership the organization gained deeper insight into actionable strategies to achieve a faster transformation.

Insight Gained:

The scores across departments varied. What we did learn is that those departments who had experienced change leadership and adaptability training had higher scores than those who had yet to develop such skills.

To achieve its goals of creating a change ready culture the organization committed to growing its skills in change leaders, adaptability, and agility.

As you read the case study below, you might see how the development of change leadership, adaptability, and agility played a pivotal role in resolving a critical organizational challenge.

The Problem:

Rockland prided itself on its customer service. Internally they built a Center of Excellence dedicated to customer experience. Year after year they surveyed their customers and year by year the scores began to slide. The differential was so little that the organization, in its busyness, put the results aside. Over time the reductions added up and suddenly senior leadership labeled this concern a top priority. How could customer experience erode given it was their core value? The answer is easy to understand. How many times have you walked through the lobby of an organization who has a mission statement on its wall or its core values in bold letters not to have the experience modeled at the reception desk? Unless the values become operationalized, measured and reported their impact is easily lost.

The organization did what most organizations do first, they tried to collect data. They surveyed their customers, they held internal focus groups, they asked for input from their employees. The feedback from their customers had gotten uglier. They felt the organization was not equipped to meet their needs as quickly as needed, was not receptive to change and was falling behind in living up to the standards expected. The focus groups held over a period of time revealed concerns from lack of information, communication problems, conflict with customer support team members, lack of consistency in responses and reduced escalation and prioritization. They also felt the organization in its growth had become too bureaucratic and failed to understand the news of their business. Ouch.

The Impact:

- A decline in customer satisfaction
- Loss of market share
- Financial loss
- Misalignment between leadership aspiration and operational function
- Reduced employee morale of hard-working employees surprised by customer feedback.

Rockland did what most organizations would do, they gathered the data, condensed it to key priorities and presented it to upper management. Their power point presentation was concise and professionally presented in the boardroom, and well attended by senior leadership. The problem was there appeared to be too many priorities that would take too many resources and leadership was unsure what would produce the fastest outcome. There also wasn't a measurement of the financial and business impact of the problem or the opportunity for its resolution. Their challenge was, "where do we even start?"

We were already working within the organization when

this process took place. We make it a priority to tune into what is impacting our clients. Stepping forward we offered to review the data.

There is a saying that the "fish can't see the water" or another that "the sharpest knife cannot carve its own handle." That is the benefit of an outside organization. Often because we are not in the vortex of the organization, we can quickly see root causes and solutions.

The Need:

In our strategic asset review we read through all the internal documents, the customer surveys, the focus group results, and interviewed leadership and key stakeholders. We identified the department that would have the biggest impact in lifting customer satisfaction. The same department had also developed through Changeability skill building the year prior. We used scientific data to laser focus on the key areas that would improve scores. Our customers are busy, they are putting out daily dumpster fires while trying to stay ahead, we try our best to provide laser focused solutions that provide quick wins yet sustainable results.

In the midst of the data, what stood out to me so clearly was the customer's perception of the customer service team. They were viewed as a support team instead of a strategic partner to the success of their business. A function instead of a partner. What I know from having worked within many organizations is that partnership relationships are often the key to success. When you view your customers, vendors, suppliers, and colleague departments as partners, the relationship changes. I noted the need for a shift in perspective both from the customer's view and how the department viewed themselves.

Secondly, we looked at the organization's data collection and our own data science. What would drive an increase in customer satisfaction and do so with predictable results? We identified the key areas needed by the department. In order to meet the demands of the customer and to also shift from being viewed as a function to a that of a strategic partner we would focus on increasing their Growth Mindset, their ability to Embrace Change, build Trust with their customers, increase their capacity to manage Conflict, and to provide improved access and consistency in information and in response time. The problem was while employees viewed themselves as proficient in these areas, the customers had a different perspective.

Our study assessed key competencies for delivering exceptional customer experiences. Employees' self-evaluations exceeded customers' ratings, indicating a perception gap. Each competency's findings are detailed in this report.

Scale

5: True to my experience
4: Somewhat true
3: Neither true or untrue
2: Somewhat true of my experience
1: Untrue of my experience

Results

Conflict Resolution

1. I strive to amicably resolve customers' concerns:
   Employee Rating: 5.0
   Customer Rating: 4.19

Debora J. McLaughlin

2. I look for win-win solutions:
   Employee Rating: 5.0
   Customer Rating: 3.06

3. I handle challenges well:
   Employee Rating: 4.25
   Customer Rating: 3.06

Trust Building

1. I demonstrate confidence in delivering services that meet customers' needs:
   Employee Rating: 4.75
   Customer Rating: 3.63

2. I show clients I have their best interest in mind:
   Employee Rating: 4.5
   Customer Rating: 3.5

Information Sharing

1. I provide customers with the information they need in time to put to use:
   Employee Rating: 4.88
   Customer Rating: 3.5

2. I provide access to information so customers can make decisions:
   Employee Rating: 4.88
   Customer Rating: 3.06

Growth Mindset

1. I approach problems with an optimistic outlook:
   Employee Rating: 3.88
   Customer Rating: 2.04

2. I am open to new ideas and approaches:
   Employee Rating: 4.75
   Customer Rating: 2.75

3. I am willing to learn new ways of doing things:
   Employee Rating: 4.88
   Customer Rating: 2.23

Embrace Change

1. I update outdated policies and practices:
   Employee Rating: 4
   Customer Rating: 1.6

The results show that employees rate their competencies higher than customers. Successful organizations use customer feedback to develop the skills to enhance satisfaction and effective service delivery.

The Solution:

By building a more strategic relationship with their customers our goal was to increase customer satisfaction scores while strengthening employee competencies.

We try to limit the resources needed so we gathered a small

subset of the organization into an Action Focus Group. The intent of such a group is to solve a problem or to maximize an opportunity. In this case, we focused on improving customer satisfaction. Our goal is also to strengthen the skills of participants. In the process they learn about each other, overcome communication gaps in the team, see each other's strengths, identify team gaps and focus on building a business case or production business results. The data was presented, and the coaching consulting refined to skill building in the identified areas as well as the shifts in mental flexibility, mindset, adaptability, and brand perception of themselves as well as identifying what an ideal partnership might look like with their customers.

The team aimed to improve customer service by shifting from reactive responses to proactive, consultative partnerships. They envisioned a new relationship with customers that focused on meeting and anticipating their needs. This transformative approach required stepping out of their comfort zones and embracing new strategies for change leadership, communication, and conflict management.

The team developed the skills needed to become strategic partners through training and coaching. They adopted a growth mindset, unlearned outdated processes, and embraced new customer communication methods. Because this team already had the skill set of Changeability, we could produce faster results.

Action and experimentation is the only way learning can become part of the fabric of the organization's culture. To activate this the team did something they had never done before, they began to schedule meetings with customers, not to support a current transaction but to better understand their business and for the customer to understand their role as their success partner. This shift from transactional partner to transformational partner wasn't easy for all participants. For some it was intimidating, while others were excited about the opportunity to show their value. We supported each individual catering to their unique needs; however all were to complete the task.

Now with a clearly defined plan and brand message they scheduled meetings, positioning themselves as strategic partners rather than a transactional support team.

Results:

The study resulted in team members connecting with their customers in a new way, talking not about projects and progress but about the customers' business goals, challenges, and ways to strategically partner together for positive business results. Together, they discovered new, creative ways to strategically partner and deliver positive business results.

Team members began to build trust with their internal customer partners. That trust turned into the team sharing the different ways they could be of service to one another, working towards collective improvements—together. The results began to add up, offering cost, time, and energy savings, and replacing frustration with partnership.

They used a communication skill-based approach. As they interacted their confidence expanded. They were seen by their customers as their success partner and were invited to attend critical customer meetings more often. Productivity improved. Engagement improved. Customers reported great improvements in their unsolicited feedback to senior leadership. Customer satisfaction improved.

Our client's investment matters and as part of every

engagement we measure and report on success metrics and the return of investment.

Did the team acquire new skills? Did the customer experience improve?

Customer's Rank and Increase in Team's Competency: The team's growth in adaptability skills, such as conflict resolution, embracing change, growth mindset, information access, and trust, was assessed through pre- and post-surveys. The ratings provided by customers demonstrated the improvements achieved.

Overall, customers reported an increase in all competencies measured. Employees rated the skills and experience as positive, indicating their own growth. They saw themselves as strategic partners who add value and were valued by their customers.

In the areas of conflict, embracing change, growth mindset, information access, and trust, customers saw significant growth. One customer stated, "I notice that the responses are less transactional and process-oriented, and more focused on how we can solve the problem."

Measurable Results in 90 days:

Customer Satisfaction increases specifically defined as a:

- 66% increase in demonstrated ability to handle challenges
- 33% increase in looking for win-win solutions
- 67% increase in showing an interest in problem solving
- 56% increase in ability to solve problems
- 66% increase in being better positioned to handle challenges
- 36% increase in access to information

- 33% increase in being willing to learn new things
- 56% increase in confidence in service delivery

Timeframe: 90 Days

Your investment matters; that is why we also measure the impact and return on investment of every engagement. ROI: Rockland's validated ROI of 162% return of investment of the engagement.

Why Did It Work?

Data was used to drive decisions. Through assessment and strategic analysis we were able to deliver a solution that offered predictable results. The analysis determined and streamlined the training, coaching and consulting needed to provide the desired outcome.

The engagement succeeded because the team members learned how to connect with their customers in a new way. They arrived at the meetings ready to have strategic supportive business meetings. Instead of talking about projects, services and progress as they might have in the past, they talked about the customer's goals, challenges and ways to strategically partner together to achieve results. The team used their new learned skills of change leadership and adaptability to not only shift their own perspective of the client but to also shift the customer's perspective of the team.

This required a shift in mindset and mental flexibility.

They recrafted their communication plan to include head, heart and hand discussions; these change leadership strategies enabled them to engage, enroll and align with their customers more easily.

Team members asked questions of their customer partners, listened intently to their needs and sought win-win solutions to solve problems. These actions created trust and developed proactive partnership, all the while helping to avoid conflicts.

Customers began to engage with the organization sooner and grew in their level of trust. Team members were seen as success partners to their business.

Together customers and team members found better ways to work together, and these relationships resulted in time savings, increased productivity and financial gains.

Rockland's biggest risk was the loss of their customers' trust. Their vision of operationalizing a center of excellence had come to fruition.

Equipped with enhanced competencies, the team became future-ready for changes and disruptions. Recognizing the success, the organization continued the process, fostering innovation teams in other departments and creating a sustainable cultural shift.

This case study exemplifies that adaptability is not merely a frame of mind but a set of learnable and enhanced abilities, character traits, and environmental characteristics. By combining these elements and following a structured process, organizations can improve their ability to navigate change, drive innovation, and thrive in an ever-evolving work landscape.

Changeability was embraced as a mindset and a strategic imperative. The organization recognized the need to adapt to digital disruption and shift from a tactical focus to strategic collaboration. By fostering a culture of change leadership, the team was empowered to drive positive change and innovation proactively.

Change leadership was a guiding force throughout the

transformation. The department's leader championed bringing change leadership and adaptability into the organization. The team leaders and members demonstrated the ability to envision a new customer relationship paradigm, challenge the status quo, and inspire others to embrace the vision. They facilitated the necessary shifts in mindset and behaviors, ensuring everyone understood the importance of building strong customer partnerships.

Adaptability was essential in navigating the challenges and uncertainties during the transformation process. The team members cultivated a growth mindset, embracing new ideas, learning, and unlearning old habits. They were willing to step outside their comfort zones, try new approaches, and continuously improve their skills and competencies. This adaptability allowed them to respond effectively to changing circumstances and customer needs.

Agility was a crucial factor in the team's success. This agility enabled them to overcome obstacles, maintain productivity, and deliver results within the 90-day timeframe.

Through Changeability: change leadership, adaptability, and agility, the team transformed their approach from transactional to transformational. They focused on building strategic partnerships, understanding customer needs, and delivering proactive solutions. The results were remarkable, with improvements in every measured competency, increased customer satisfaction, higher Net Promoter Scores, and a significant return on investment. "We soon were receiving accolades from the business, asking our team to be at the table, to be involved in decisions where we could have the greatest influence," the team's senior leader reported.

One year later, this team continues to improve and innovate. While other departments are facing attrition, this team remains intact. In addition, three team members were promoted within the organization and the department's employee engagement scores rank the highest across the organization.

This case study highlights the power of embracing change and leveraging key attributes to drive organizational success. Organizations that cultivate Changeability, foster change leadership, nurture adaptability, and embrace agility are better equipped to navigate uncertainty, respond to customer needs, and achieve their goals quickly.

In reflection, I believe the organization gained the results delivered because it had readied their employees for change. By investing in change leadership training and adaptability through assessment, coaching and consulting, the team was ready. I also know the untold truth. When given a safe space to explore employees' latent or inactivated skills for change come alive or are amplified. The 90-day action focus groups provide the experimental space for participants to leverage their strengths, to activate their underutilized, undiscovered or latent capabilities in a safe supportive environment.

I know my work is done, not only when a business problem is solved or an opportunity gained, but when I see the team members I work with inspired, growing, contributing, and being valued within their organization.

CHAPTER 10

Unleashing Possibilities

"Every great dream begins with a dreamer. Always remember, you have within you the strength, the patience, and the passion to reach for the stars to change the world."

—Harriet Tubman

I heard the commotion as soon as I returned home. A rustling was coming from upstairs.

Noticing my bedroom door was closed, I crept up the stairs quietly to investigate. I opened the door and saw my husband standing in the middle of the room. His face seemed to be in a panic. His hands were raised above his head. He held a knotted gathering of the corners of a white sheet in each of his hands.

"We have to get it!" he said. "It" was a small black bird, equally as terrified as my husband, perched on the top of our armoire. "I'm going to grab it with the sheet. You go down the stairs and open the front door, and we can get it out of here," he said.

I envisioned the process, collecting the bird in the sheet, hoping not to injure it in the process. Risking running down the stairs with the possibility the bird might wrestle its way out of the loose sheet and into the high ceilings of our grand foyer, where we would never be able to catch it. I weighed the timing of opening the door and the imagined perception of our neighbors if they saw us flinging our sheet onto the front walkway.

I walked over to the window by the armoire. "Or we could open the window," I said, reaching for the handle. I hardly finished my sentence before the bird, feeling the cool breeze, quickly exited.

And that is what Changeability is, your window.

For over twenty years, I've seen faces like my husband's. Leaders who need to provide a solution to a dumpster fire problem. Teams are charged with improving a process but need help figuring out where to start. Organizations that are so close to their culture fail to see the root cause of losing talented people or market share because they can't respond fast enough to stay ahead of their competition.

When you are trapped in a world of constant change compounded with the frustration of navigating personalities, policies, politicking, and compliance policing, it is hard to see a way through.

That is where the skill set of Changeability comes in. Think of Changeability as your window. It gives you what you need to navigate the challenge, make fast decisions, and move through obstacles.

You may share some of the same concerns as my clients. Do you?

- Desire to be seen as a good leader.
- Want your work to be valued and your organization to recognize its impact.
- Worry when deadlines start to slip, people work less effectively, or accountability erodes.
- Become excited when a high-stakes project becomes your responsibility yet secretly ponder if you can pull it off.
- Wish you could delegate more, but you worry if your team can handle the added load.
- Try to dial back the stress and gain more time to focus on what matters.
- Work hard yet long for more time for yourself and your loved ones?

If so, you are ready for changeability. I love to partner with leaders who have a vision and a determination to succeed. The world of business is changing. There will be more change around the bend that might be impossible to currently see, you have to be ready.

I've identified the key to success as Changeability. Changeability is:

The willingness to challenge what's possible.

To fully focus on uncertainty and disruption and iterate towards success.

To have the energy and confidence to explore the unknown, backed by the daring and determination to push boundaries and reimagine new paths forward.

The superpower of the modern age, enabling real and meaningful progress through audacious experimentation.

Yet despite having a vision you might have obstacles that get in your way. Let's kick them to the curb.

So how do you get started? Let's review the journey.

You read why Changeability is critical and how its three components, change leadership, adaptability, and agility work together. All attributes were demonstrated in the case study.

You may have resonated with some of the struggles incurred in the client stories. Dave took on an enterprise digital transformation that challenged his team and was a pivotal point in his career. You learned how your perceptions may affect their performance in the story of Randy and how his shift in mindset elevated not only his team's performance but his own visibility within the organization, leading to a promotion. Randy's story focuses on letting go to move forward and unlearning old beliefs. Letting go of biases, distrust, and micromanaging to shift into a change leadership style allowed him to see others differently. Deeply rooted in his control style of leadership, it wasn't easy to loosen the reins. However, when he learned how to communicate as a change leader and increase accountability through coaching, he gained the time to focus on more strategic projects. Shahanna was surprised by the resistance of her talented team and through a revised emphasis on adaptability she was quickly able to re-engage them. Raj balanced the organization's focus on their legacy products with his personal and professional vision for growth. Raj honed new skills to influence others to navigate policy, politics, and resistance.

So, what do all these stories have in common?

Throughout, it was obvious no one could do it alone. But it is not as if they didn't try. But they were stuck, like the bird unable to see a new way out.

With an outside perspective, they were able to open their mind to a new possibility. Their lens for opportunity was widened once they could step away from the comfort zone of "what's always worked" into the adaptability zone of "let's try something new." New ideas sparked their creativity, fueling innovation. They shifted from holding onto what they knew to leveling up their skills with new learning, and new learning birthed greater creativity, curiosity, and energy.

In our engagements, we embed the "just in time" skills needed, whether it be improving team effectiveness, speeding the implementation of a change by engaging and enrolling others to speed adoption, building a culture that instills a sense of belonging, trust and psychological safety or reframing communication to have more successful conversations.

As demonstrated in their stories, our clients are viewed as distinguished leaders. Some chose to become change catalysts. They amplified their growth mindset and ability to embrace change, instill trust, and communicate in a way that engaged, enrolled, and empowered others. As a result, their influence grew, and they soon made process improvements while practicing risk intelligence. In addition, they suggested innovations to improve customer satisfaction and reclaimed market positioning.

Others took a more inward focus. With new skills, they saw the potential and possibility in their team. They grew confident in their team's ability to accomplish more and sought out stretch projects with more significant impact. They delegated, reducing stress and freeing their time to focus on what was important to them.

All experienced a shift in thinking and behavior which might not have happened if they weren't passengers on the road to Changeability.

So how did the three components of Changeability come into play?

Change leadership will enable you to motivate, influence, and engage others. Adaptability is the ability to adjust to changing circumstances, ideas, or environments. It allows people to make changes to existing methods, technologies, or processes to make an improvement. Finally, agility enables you and your team to make fast decisions to achieve more than you think possible and with greater ease and mastery.

In each client story, not only did they deliver results, but the person they became in the process gave them the mindset, skill set, and determination to face any challenge or opportunity. As a result, they can now stand steadfast no matter what storm brews.

But what makes someone a great leader? Great leaders adapt to changes in their environment, recognize new opportunities, and empower others to succeed through courage, curiosity, and confidence through challenging circumstances. With these attributes comes certainty.

- Courage: the willingness to look for opportunities within obstacles
- Curiosity: seeing things from a different vantage point

- Confidence: the ability to take the next step even when the path isn't clear
- Certainty: the mindset of success even if the only outcome is a new learning

Being a change leader means understanding that change is inevitable and being prepared to lead change and drive results.

The Bottom Line

With Changeability, you adapt to the ever-changing demands of your environment, know how to respond to change, and transform your team members so that they can recognize, respond to, and strive in the face of change. The first step is to take action.

The Renegade Leader Amplification™ process which has been proven to be successful for over two decades includes:

Assess: Here we illuminate your goals, the current state, and desired outcomes.

Align: We align to the goals including competencies, success metrics, timeline and expected results, generating a cohesive and collaborative roadmap.

Activate: We implement the assessments, coaching, training, and agreed upon services in the consulting plan. We meet with clients, sponsors, and executives continuously to monitor progress and alignment.

Accelerate/Amplify: My favorite delivery, amplifying results. Our clients gain unexpected results, business results greater than what might have been expected, and they transform personally and professionally.

As you read in the case studies, they are able to lead with greater confidence and ease. Time becomes manageable. They gain space to think and spend time with their loved ones. They are motivated and transformed, different in many positive ways. The shift in mindset leads to greater expansiveness. Imagine being able to have more time to yourself, to be recognized as a valued leader and a leader others choose to follow. Many are promoted because they have established greater personal and professional networks and are more known within their organization or perhaps even their industry. From this new vantage point, you can see opportunities and to see what is possible for yourself, your team and your organization. A true change catalyst.

Assess: Your investment matters. That is why we measure and report the ROI of our engagements against the verified success metrics defined.

This book is information, only action leads to transformation.

*"90 percent of executives recognize the need to act on
their organization's capability to grow, but only 5 percent
believe they already have the capabilities required."*
McKinsey, State of Organizations 2023

There are four ways we work with leaders, teams and organizations.

Build your ability to coach and lead your team through change. Through AI coaching and personalized coaching we build a coaching plan around your goals.

If you are facing change or have key priorities within the next 90 days, I invite you to have a conversation. Having gained insight across industries and thousands of leaders, I've seen what works and what doesn't. I want you to avoid anything that might slow you down or get in the way of your success. In this launch meeting I'll listen to your goals and your challenges and provide at least three strategies for quick wins or to gain traction. You will leave our meeting with a plan to put into action.

If you are ready to gain insight into your team's degree of change readiness with measurements at the individual and team level, I invite you to assess your team's Changeability. Prior to the assessment we will meet to identify your current goals and priorities. I will analyze the data and align the results to your current goals. In your executive debriefing you will learn how to leverage the skillset, mindset, and adaptability of your team to accelerate successful business outcomes.

Want to involve your team? Great, we will debrief and train your team on how to leverage its strengths and bridge gaps quickly and easily.

Ready to build a change ready organization? Together we will identify your competency and business goals and through assessment, coaching and training build the model to achieve those goals. We don't believe in building codependency, instead we build the confidence, capacity and capabilities for your organization to navigate, initiate and lead change with conviction and confidence.

The Truth

Remember the bird in the house? I never told my husband the truth about the bird, nor did he think to ask. It was a late fall day, and all of our screens had been removed for the winter season. Worrying about an interruption from my three golden retrievers during a zoom call, I left the kitchen slider door open so the trio could come and go safely within the confines of our invisible fence system.

I failed to imagine anything else coming through the slider door. Instead, I focused on my work. And that is when we miss what might be possible. When our head is down in the trenches. When we are too nearsighted to see the fuller possibility. I love what I do, empowering clients to see new possibilities and making them their reality. Using the strategies outlined here, you can strengthen your skillset of Changeability, and you will find it gives you the freedom to lead your team effectively with less time, energy, and bandwidth.

Imagine you and your team can weather any storm that comes your way, digital disruption, market competition, a multigenerational workforce with diverse needs, shifting customer demands, the need for innovation, and the exponential speed of change. The problems and opportunities will come and go; the difference will be you and your team will be ready. You can have the capacity to not only navigate change but to initiate it.

The future isn't scary if you are the one creating it. It is my hope that you take the step to lead forward, with unwavering conviction, forging a path towards a future that you shape and define.

Forward Action:

1. **Join me on <u>LinkedIn</u>**

   Keep current on current strategies and tune into our Client Dilemma series, offering the latest solutions to problems you can relate to.

2. **Let's Connect!**

   Let's connect for a conversation, bring your goal, challenges, and opportunities, and leave with up to three strategies you can immediately put into action. You can self-schedule at <u>www.SchedulewithDebora.com</u>

3. **Work with my team or me privately**

   Changeability is measurable. Would it be helpful to know your team or organization's change readiness score or reskill index? Learn how to leverage strengths, bridge gaps and how to build a future ready culture. Step to the edge of possibility and see what is possible for you, your team, or your organization. Start with the conversation, <u>www.SchedulewithDebora.com</u> email <u>Debora@theRenegadeLeader.com</u> or give us a call.

4. **Join the Changeability Accelerator Initiative**

   Available Changeability Assessments with Strategic Debrief: Assess your Change Readiness: Change Leadership, Adaptability and Agility and discover your or your team/organizations change readiness.

Change Intelligence will offer insight to change leadership and identify head, heart and hand strengths. AQ®, Adaptability Quotient, serves as a comprehensive gauge of adaptability within the workplace. A higher AQ® signifies a greater likelihood for you and your team to bounce back from setbacks, innovate alternative solutions to challenges, and wholeheartedly embrace change. PQ, or positive intelligence also supports the shifts needed to raise the performance of any team. Assessments can be confusing, let us pick which one is right for you to turbo charge your results. Contact us to learn more.

Let your success story be the next one!

ABOUT THE AUTHOR

As CEO of The Renegade Leader Coaching and Consulting Group, Debora McLaughlin and her team work with executives and leadership teams to maximize their leadership success, create high-performing future-ready teams, and grow and strategically differentiate their business through consulting, executive coaching, assessments, leadership development, business coaching, and organizational consulting.

Debora is the author of Amazon bestsellers, *The Renegade Leader, 9 Success Strategies Driven Leaders Use to Ignite People, Performance and Profits* and *Running in High Heels, How to Lead with Influence, Impact, and Ingenuity.* She is co-author of *Blueprint for Success, Proven Strategies for Success and Survival* with Stephen M. R. Covey and Ken Blanchard, and *The Roadmap for Career Success* with Lisa Martelli. She is a featured contributor to other anthologies and is referenced as one of Corporate America's most requested coaches in *Straight Talk for Getting Results and No Winner Ever Got There Without A Coach.*

An ICF Professional Certified Executive Coach, Debora uniquely combines 25 years of real-world experience and expertise in consulting, coaching, psychology, and neuroscience with advanced certifications in multicultural diversity, change leadership, adaptability, executive coaching, and business coaching.

She holds two Master of Arts degrees from Hunter College, New York City, and Rivier University and a Bachelor of Arts in Psychology from Franklin Pierce University.

Her clients include Fortune 500 companies and for-profit organizations in Technology, Finance, Healthcare, Insurance, Manufacturing, Hospitality, and Retail.

Known for her keen ability to crack the code on human dynamics, Debora enables leaders to get the desired results by inoculating organizations against distrust, fear, lack of accountability, and disorganization. Instead, she builds collaborative cultures of engaged, energized, and spirited employees led by confident, innovative leaders. Her dynamic personality and willingness to share the truth make her a valued mentor, giving the bright leaders she works with the specific tools and support they need to succeed. As a result, many of her clients have been able to grow award-winning companies, increase their profits, and receive recognition and promotion for their leadership roles.

Debora's thought leadership is found in media such as Leadership Excellence, Yahoo Finance, IT Business Net, American Management Association, Money Watch, Boston Harold, Inc. Magazine, Forbes, The Wall Street Journal, and others.

In addition to her consulting work, Debora is a mentor and advisor for forward-thinking innovators such as AQai.io and Excelia.io. She is a founding member of the Genius Think Tank, which is comprised of business leaders across industries. She is dedicated to continuous learning and staying abreast of the latest research and trends, ensuring her clients receive the most up-to-date and impactful guidance.

Her ultimate goal is to create profitable organizations that are successful and great places to work, fostering cultures of passion, energy, and innovation. By working with Debora as a Renegade Leader, you'll amplify what's possible in your business and personal visions and gain the ability to inspire your team and drive positive change. Leadership is challenging, but with Changeability, you can become a leader known for their ability to deliver transformative results.

Contact Us
The Renegade Leader Coaching and Consulting Group
603-324-7171
www.TheRenegadeLeader.com
Debora@TheRenegadeLeader.com

THE *R*ENEGADE *L*EADER®
COACHING & CONSULTING GROUP

RESOURCES

Reports:

- World Economic Forum, "The Future of Jobs Report 2020,"

  https://www.weforum.org/reports/the-future-of-jobs-report-2020. According to a study by the World Economic Forum, the top 10 skills that employees will need by 2025 include "resilience, stress tolerance, and flexibility" to adapt to the rapidly changing world of work.

- McKinsey & Company, "Are You Adaptable Enough to Thrive in the New World of Work?

  https://www.mckinsey.com/business-functions/organization/our-insights/are-you-adaptable-enough-to-thrive-in-the-new-world-of-work. A McKinsey survey found that companies prioritizing adaptability outperformed their less adaptable peers by 1.8 times in revenue growth and 2.0 times in total shareholder return.

- Deloitte, "The Rise of the Social Enterprise,"

  https://www2.deloitte.com/content/dam/insights/us/articles/HCTrends-2019/DI_HC-Trends-2019.pdf.

- PwC, "Eight Essential Elements of a High-Performance Business Culture,"

  https://www.pwc.com/gx/en/services/people-organisation/publications/high-performance-culture.html. A report by PwC found that 79% of business leaders believe that the ability to adapt to change is a "key driver of success" for their organization.

- Society for Human Resource Management (SHRM), "2020 Competency Model,"

  https://www.shrm.org/hr-today/trends-and-forecasting/research-and-surveys/documents/2020-shrm-competency-model-competencies-and-behaviors.pdf.

- Agile Alliance. (2020). State of Agile Report 2020. https://www.agilealliance.org/state-of-agile-report/
- Agile Alliance. (2020). State of Agile Report 2020. https://www.agilealliance.org/state-of-agile-report/

Adaptability

3rd party articles and studies on Adaptability

- Gao, X., Xin, X., Zhou, W., & Jepsen, D. M. (2019). Combine Your "Will" and "Able": Career Adaptability's Influence on Performance. Frontiers in Psychology.

Agile Alliance. (2020). State of Agile Report 2020. https://www.agilealliance.org/state-of-agile-report/

- Deloitte, "The Rise of the Social Enterprise," https://www2.deloitte.com/content/dam/insights/us/articles/HCTrends-2019/DI_HC-Trends-2019.pdf.

- McKinsey & Company, "Are You Adaptable Enough to Thrive in the New World of Work?" https://www.mckinsey.com/business-functions/organization/our-insights/are-you-adaptable-enough-to-thrive-in-the-new-world-of-work.

- PwC, "Eight Essential Elements of a High-Performance Business Culture," https://www.pwc.com/gx/en/services/people-organisation/publications/high-performance-culture.html.

- Society for Human Resource Management (SHRM), "2020 Competency Model," https://www.shrm.org/hr-today/trends-and-forecasting/research-and-surveys/documents/2020-shrm-competency-model-competencies-and-behaviors.pdf.

- World Economic Forum, "The Future of Jobs Report 2020," https://www.weforum.org/reports/the-future-of-jobs-report-2020

- Howard, J. L., Gagné, M., & Bureau, J. S. (2017b). Testing a continuum structure of self-determined motivation: A meta-analysis. Psychological Bulletin, 143(12), 1346–1377. https://doi.org/10.1037/bul0000125

- Kuntz, J., Malinen, S., & Näswall, K. (2017). Employee resilience: Directions for resilience development. Consulting Psychology Journal: Practice and Research, 69(3), 223–242. https://doi.org/10.1037/cpb0000097

- Marinova, S. V., Peng, C., Lorinkova, N., Van Dyne, L., & Chiaburu, D. S. (2015). Change-oriented behavior:

A meta-analysis of individual and job design predictors. Journal of Vocational Behavior, 88, 104–120. https://doi.org/10.1016/j.jvb.2015.02.006

- Nedelkoska, Ljubica,, Quintini, Glenda. Automation, skills use and training. OECD Social, Employment and Migration Working Papers. (2018). OECD Social Employment and Migration Working Papers. https://doi.org/10.1787/1815199x
- Oglesby, M. E., Allan, N. P., Short, N. A., Raines, A. M., & Schmidt, N. B. (2017). Factor mixture modeling of intolerance of uncertainty. Psychological Assessment, 29(4), 435–445. https://doi.org/10.1037/pas0000357
- Petrou, P., Demerouti, E., & Schaufeli, W. B. (2018b). Crafting the Change: The Role of Employee Job Crafting Behaviors for Successful Organizational Change. Journal of Management, 44(5), 1766–1792. https://doi.org/10.1177/0149206315624961
- Rudolph, C. W., Lavigne, K. N., & Zacher, H. (2017b). Career adaptability: A meta-analysis of relationships with measures of adaptivity, adapting responses, and adaptation results. Journal of Vocational Behavior, 98, 17–34. https://doi.org/10.1016/j.jvb.2016.09.002
- Tabibnia, G., & Radecki, D. (2018b). Resilience training that can change the brain. Consulting Psychology Journal: Practice and Research, 70(1), 59–88. https://doi.org/10.1037/cpb0000110
- Uhl-Bien, M., & Arena, M. J. (2018b). Leadership for organizational adaptability: A theoretical synthesis and integrative framework. Leadership Quarterly, 29(1), 89–104. https://doi.org/10.1016/j.leaqua.2017.12.009
- Ullén, F., Hambrick, D. Z., & Mosing, M. A. (2016b). Rethinking expertise: A multifactorial

gene–environment interaction model of expert performance. Psychological Bulletin, 142(4), 427–446. https://doi.org/10.1037/bul0000033

- Van Steenbergen, E. F., Van Der Ven, C. M., Peeters, M. C. W., & Taris, T. W. (2018). Transitioning Towards New Ways of Working: Do Job Demands, Job Resources, Burnout, and Engagement Change? Psychological Reports, 121(4), 736–766. https://doi.org/10.1177/0033294117740134
- Zingoni, M., & Corey, C. M. (2017b). How Mindset Matters. Journal of Personnel Psychology, 16(1), 36–45. https://doi.org/10.1027/1866-5888/a000171

Agility

3rd party articles and studies on the application and outcomes of Agility

- Cai, Z., Parker, S. K., Li, S., & Lam, W. (2019b). How does the social context fuel the proactive fire? A multilevel review and theoretical synthesis. Journal of Organizational Behavior, 40(2), 209–230. https://doi.org/10.1002/job.2347
- Meuse, D., & Kenneth, P. (2017b). Learning agility: Its evolution as a psychological construct and its empirical relationship to leader success. Consulting Psychology Journal: Practice and Research, 69(4), 267–295. https://doi.org/10.1037/cpb0000100
- Rudolph, C. W., Katz, I. M., Lavigne, K. N., & Zacher, H. (2017b). Job crafting: A meta-analysis of relationships with individual differences, job characteristics, and

work outcomes. Journal of Vocational Behavior, 102, 112–138. https://doi.org/10.1016/j.jvb.2017.05.008

- Shoji, K., Cieslak, R., Smoktunowicz, E., Rogala, A., Benight, C. C., & Luszczynska, A. (2016b). Associations between job burnout and self-efficacy: a meta-analysis. Anxiety Stress and Coping, 29(4), 367–386. https://doi.org/10.1080/10615806.2015.1058369

Change

3rd party articles and studies on the application and outcomes of Change

- Berkman, E. T. (2018b). The neuroscience of goals and behavior change. Consulting Psychology Journal: Practice and Research, 70(1), 28–44. https://doi.org/10.1037/cpb0000094
- Fasbender, U., Wöhrmann, A. M., Wang, M., & Klehe, U. (2019b). Is the future still open? The mediating role of occupational future time perspective in the effects of career adaptability and aging experience on late career planning. Journal of Vocational Behavior, 111, 24–38. https://doi.org/10.1016/j.jvb.2018.10.006

Wellbeing

3rd party articles and studies on the application and outcomes for Wellbeing

- Kun, B., Urbán, R., Paksi, B., Csóbor, L. V., Oláh, A., & Demetrovics, Z. (2012). Psychometric characteristics of the Emotional Quotient Inventory, Youth Version,

Short Form, in Hungarian high school students. Psychological Assessment, 24(2), 518–523. https://doi. org/10.1037/a0026013

- Parker, J. D. A., Keefer, K. V., & Wood, L. D. (2011b). Toward a brief multidimensional assessment of emotional intelligence: Psychometric properties of the Emotional Quotient Inventory—Short Form. Psychological Assessment, 23(3), 762–777. https://doi. org/10.1037/a0023289
- Thundiyil, T., Chiaburu, D. S., Banks, G. C., & Peng, A. C. (2014). Cynical about Change? A Meta-Analysis of Organizational Cynicism Correlates. Proceedings - Academy of Management. https://doi. org/10.5465/ambpp.2014.177
- Rodríguez-Rey, R., Alonso-Tapia, J., & Garrido-Hernansaiz, H. (2016b). Reliability and validity of the Brief Resilience Scale (BRS) Spanish Version. Psychological Assessment, 28(5), e101–e110. https://doi. org/10.1037/pas0000191
- Seidel, J. A., Andrews, W. W., Owen, J., Carreira, E. M., & Buccino, D. L. (2017). Preliminary validation of the Rating of Outcome Scale and equivalence of ultra-brief measures of well-being. Psychological Assessment, 29(1), 65–75. https://doi.org/10.1037/pas0000311

Personality

3rd party articles and studies on Personality

- Burnette, J. L., O'Boyle, E. H., VanEpps, E. M., Pollack, J. M., & Finkel, E. J. (2013). Mind-sets matter: A meta-analytic review of implicit theories and self-regulation.

Psychological Bulletin, 139(3), 655–701. https://doi.
org/10.1037/a0029531

- Major, D. A., Turner, J. H., & Fletcher, T. H. (2006).
Linking proactive personality and the Big Five to
motivation to learn and development activity. Journal
of Applied Psychology, 91(4), 927–935. https://doi.
org/10.1037/0021-9010.91.4.927

- Rammstedt, B., & John, O. P. (2007). Measuring
personality in one minute or less: A 10-item short
version of the Big Five Inventory in English and
German. Journal of Research in Personality, 41(1),
203–212. https://doi.org/10.1016/j.jrp.2006.02.001

- Usher, E. L., Li, C., Butz, A. R., & Rojas, J. P. (2019).
Perseverant grit and self-efficacy: Are both essential
for children's academic success? Journal of Educational
Psychology, 111(5), 877–902. https://doi.org/10.1037/
edu0000324

- Van Der Linden, D., Pekaar, K. A., Bakker, A. B.,
Schermer, J. A., Vernon, P. A., Dunkel, C. S., &
Petrides, K. V. (2017b). Overlap between the general
factor of personality and emotional intelligence: A
meta-analysis. Psychological Bulletin, 143(1), 36–52.
https://doi.org/10.1037/bul0000078

- Von Culin, K. R., Tsukayama, E., & Duckworth, A.
L. (2014). Unpacking grit: Motivational correlates of
perseverance and passion for long-term goals. The
Journal of Positive Psychology, 9(4), 306–312. https://
doi.org/10.1080/17439760.2014.898320

Environment

3rd party articles and studies on Environment

- Rhoades, L., & Eisenberger, R. (2002). Perceived organizational support: A review of the literature. Journal of Applied Psychology, 87(4), 698–714. https://doi.org/10.1037/0021-9010.87.4.698
- Kurtessis, J. N., Eisenberger, R., Ford, M. J., Buffardi, L. C., Stewart, K., & Adis, C. (2017). Perceived Organizational Support: A Meta-Analytic Evaluation of Organizational Support Theory. Journal of Management, 43(6), 1854–1884. https://doi.org/10.1177/0149206315575554
- Hoch, J. E., Bommer, W. H., Dulebohn, J. H., & Wu, D. (2018). Do Ethical, Authentic, and Servant Leadership Explain Variance Above and Beyond Transformational Leadership? A Meta-Analysis. Journal of Management, 44(2), 501–529. https://doi.org/10.1177/0149206316665461

NOTES

NOTES